T5-AWJ-741

THE GOLDEN BOOK OF PRAYER

An Anthology of Prayer

EDITED BY
DONALD B. ALDRICH
IN COLLABORATION WITH
WILLIAM OLIVER STEVENS

DODD, MEAD & COMPANY
New York · 1941

FIRST EDITION

PRINTED IN THE UNITED STATES OF AMERICA
BY THE VAIL-BALLOU PRESS, INC., BINGHAMTON, N. Y.

In continuing gratitude

to

EDMUND S. ROUSMANIERE

The first Dean

of

The Cathedral Church of St. Paul, Boston

Who gave to his younger colleagues

a Hope like his own

ACKNOWLEDGMENTS

The author and the editors of THE GOLDEN BOOK OF PRAYER wish to express their sincere gratitude to the authors and publishers who kindly permitted the reprinting of their copyrighted material in this volume. Grateful acknowledgment for permission to use their selections is due to the following:

The Christian Century Press: For a prayer by Allen A. Stockdal, *beginning,* "Dear Lord of Courage and Fortitude . . ."

Contrafraternity of the Precious Blood: For "A Good-night Blessing," from MY SUNDAY MISSAL, by Rev. Joseph F. Stedman.

E. P. Dutton and Company: For a prayer from THE KINGDOM OF GOD, a play by G. Martinez Sierra. Also for selections from THE TEMPLE, by W. E. Orchard.

The Forward Movement of the Episcopal Church: For selections from PRAYERS NEW AND OLD, compiled by E. S. Rousmaniere, and published at Sharon, Pennsylvania.

Good Housekeeping: For "Mother Prayer," by Margaret Widdemer, from the issue of September, 1915.

Houghton Mifflin Company: For "A Prayer," by Alice Cary, *and* "The Fool's Prayer," by Edward Rowland Sill. Reprinted by permission.

The Macmillan Company: For excerpt from "Litany on the Grace of Childhood," "For Peace in the World," *and* "O, God, Who hast drawn over weary day," all from ACTS OF DEVOTION. "Evening Prayer," by Jakob Boehme, *and* "Prayer for Heavenly Wisdom," by Boethius, from CITY WITHOUT WALLS, by Osgood. "Day After Day," "In one Salutation," "Life of My

Life," "This is my prayer," *and* "Time is endless," all from Gitanjali, by Sir Rabindranath Tagore. Also, "D'Avalos' Prayer," from Poems, by John Masefield. By permission of The Macmillan Company, Publishers.

Virgil Markham: For a prayer by Edwin Markham, *beginning,* "Teach me Father how to go . . ." Reprinted by permission.

A. C. McClurg & Co.: For "Hymn to Ammon Ra," "In Heaven Who is Great?" (Assyrian), "Invocation to Ormazd" (Persian), "Mohammedan Prayer of Adoration," *and* "One in Spirit" (Chinese Liturgy), all from Pagan Prayers.

New York Herald Tribune: For "Give me Thy Grace," by Frederick Van de Water, reprinted by permission of the author.

Charles Scribner's Sons: For "The Land," by Maxwell Struthers Burt; a prayer form Abe Lincoln in Illinois, a play by Robert Emmet Sherwood; "A Family Prayer," by Robert Louis Stevenson, from the Thistle Edition of Stevenson; *and* a prayer, "O, Lord of Courage grave," from the Works of John Galsworthy.

INTRODUCTION

I. PREFACE

IN the happy search through the literature of prayer, the editors of this book have been guided by the desire to find prayers representative of high human aspiration from whatever source. They have selected prayers which represent every age. The selections express the inspiration of some pagan thought, the deep spiritual feeling of Hebraic faith, and the richness of Christian experience. Many of the Psalms and a number of hymns from the treasury of Christian hymnology naturally find their place in such a book of devotions. In all their choosing it is the lay reader rather than the cleric whom the editors have had in mind.

The compilers have felt that the universal impulse to pray might be encouraged by a knowledge of the setting and personal circumstances connected with certain petitions. In some cases this biographical sketch will attend the prayer itself.

The editors have tried to assemble an anthology which is fairly representative of a unique, spiritual phase of the world's literature. And, whether the petition was expressed by saint or sinner, each one should typify the essence of real prayer, the selfless aspiration of a human soul toward his God.

The editors would express their obligation to many friends who have given this venture their good counsel, especially to the Reverend Vincent L. Bennett and Dr. Edgar F. Romig. For many of the biographical sketches affixed to the prayers we are keenly indebted to the Very Reverend Henry B. Washburn, D.D. For their contribution of Occasional prayers we thank the President of the United States and Dean Wicks of Princeton. A special word of appreciation is due Mrs. Florence A. van Wyck, whose tireless industry in preparing the material has been an invaluable aid.

W. O. S.

II. WHY PRAY?

Do we not all pray, each one of us—even if not in the inherited manner of our childhood? For who is not hoping for this, or looking for that; dreading some outcome, or forestalling some failure; desiring with all his heart that some good thing come true? A doctor on his rounds, the teacher with his instinct for ideas, the social worker tireless in welfare, and every average person who wants to do his job or make himself better. "Pray without ceasing," said St. Paul. This does not suggest endless petitions and ceaseless asking. It identifies prayer with the soul's sincere desire. What we want we are always praying for. "Where your treasure is, there will your heart be also."

The skeptic might call this just wishing. The saint might warn against petition seeking to placate or to procure and ask where is the yearning to do the Will of God? It requires a long spiritual discipline and development to be sure what is the Will of God. Consequently, being human, we pray for our human needs. Where they meet with the Will of God, God answers. But answered or no, we all pray. We pray for the same reason we breathe, admitting in that act of breathing a fundamental dependency. So when we eat or think. The body must have food, the mind ideas. Since we are more than these two, our "spirit" also needs its supply. Why love? Why befriend? one might ask. Because something within us compels us to that relationship. Any honest self-scrutiny discloses this dependency, the which to acknowledge is to discover strength from beyond.

We hope the ways of this Power may be our ways. As we seriously think of the highest we know in truth, beauty, goodness, and in the superlatives of personal living, we know we cannot bend the Highest to our choice. Prayer may not affect what happens outside of us as accurately as it affects what happens within us. It can make us master what happens. It may not influence the amount of fortune or misfortune. It can provide us with an unassailable attitude with which we can meet either.

We pray, then, because it offers to life life's highest relationship. Like friendship, it releases one's self from one's self (what a welcome release!) into an experience which beckons to adventure. It is not unlike the vigor of a good game or a mountain climb or a stiff pull at the oars. Self is lost in a situation and yet in a new sense of power or of inspiration self is found. Here is the common experience of starting to do something for *our own* sake and discovering the supreme experience of doing it for *its* sake, and eventually—as we progress in this want—for *God's* sake!

Why pray? Because we are "responsive" beings. "We could not seek Thee unless Thou hadst already found us."

The Beyond out there ever beckons to the Beyond within—and with a compelling power.

D. B. A.

III. SUGGESTED USE OF THIS BOOK

Prayer, one has said, is like writing a letter to a friend. If this be a real friend, one begins not by making a series of requests. First, invariably, comes *recollection*—the face of one's friend, what he looks like, some characteristic greeting. There is a happy confidence in the certainty that he is "there" and will be glad to hear from us. "How are you?" we may begin. Then our pen moves on to recall the hours of confidence and companionship. Time and space are quite overcome by this invisible relationship.

Thereupon we may recall where we have failed in the friendship. We may seize this opportunity to admit it. For our part the confession clears the relationship. We knew our friend would understand all along and would overlook it, but we wanted to "out" with it. We feel more reconciled now to the relationship.

By now we are writing on the third page of our letter and are exceedingly happy in our relationship. We may even say so—"Thank God for the likes of you!" Thereupon we open up our minds and hearts on many matters, sharing ideas, relating news of our affairs, reminding our friend of the condition of mutual friends—their fortunes and their illnesses, our own ups and downs of circumstance.

Finally we close by assuring him that if we can do anything for him in any way to let us know and to "write soon." We want to hear from him. With a good wish we conclude our correspondence. So by our letter we have given expression to an established relationship, progressively advanced through a mutual understanding. Friendship inspires such an art and develops it. Prayer is like that. It is the art of friendship with God.

Select almost any prayer from the sections of this book in the order of:

Meditations upon the kind of Personal Spirit to Whom we may turn. (Sections I and II)
The admission of shortcomings—confessions, if you will. (Section III)
Prayers which speak of God's understanding and forgiveness. (Section III)
Prayers of gratitude. (Section IV)
Prayers of dedication. (Section V)
Prayers of one's resulting mood. (Sections VI, VII, VIII)
Intercession, and petitions for those in trouble. (Section IX)

The hope for blessings on this relationship. A leave-taking, a benediction; the good will of the Friend to carry with us. (Sections X and XI)

We feel it would be the hope of those who throughout the ages have prayed these prayers and committed them to writing that we might today find their God our Mutual Friend.

D. B. A.

TABLE OF CONTENTS

THE LORD'S PRAYER

Our Father, who art in heaven, Hallowed be thy Name. Thy kingdom come. Thy will be done, On earth as it is in heaven. Give us this day our daily bread. And forgive us our trespasses, As we forgive those who trespass against us. And lead us not into temptation, But deliver us from evil. For thine is the kingdom, and the power, and the glory, for ever and ever. Amen.

I. "BESIDE STILL WATERS"

Meditative Prayers

I. "BESIDE STILL WATERS"

MEDITATIVE PRAYERS

. . . THEREFORE it is well to let prayer be the first employment in the early morning and the last in the evening. Avoid diligently those false and deceptive thoughts which say, "wait a little, I will pray an hour hence; I must first perform this or that." For with such thoughts a man quits prayer for business, which lays hold of and entangles him so that he comes not to pray the whole day long. . . .

MARTIN LUTHER on morning and evening prayer

MEDITATION is not a mystical pastime in the Oriental sense of absorption in contemplation until one's identity is lost in the object of one's thought. Rather, to meditate is to discover the romance of solitude. "The nurse of the full-grown soul is solitude." The mystic Von Hügel advises in his letters to his niece, when she complains that her meditations do not reveal enough to her, "Cultivate your worldly interests, my dear; religion has to have something to work upon." Starry contemplation is not meditation. But to recall a sunset seen at sea, or some truth which comes out of crisis: "I must die with malice and hatred toward none," or "for their sakes I sanctify myself"; again, to remember the faith of one who would not waver, or the supporting confidence of a friend, or good will and good things which we have quite undeservedly received—

this is to voyage to far scenes of the spirit and yet to find oneself at home with oneself and one's God. Ultimately "religion is what one does with one's own solitariness." "For if the chosen soul had never been alone in deep mid-silence, open-doored to God, no greatness had ever been dreamed or done."

"Give me my scallop-shell of quiet,
My staff of faith to walk upon,
My scrip of joy, immortal diet,
My battle of salvation,
My gown of glory, hope's true gage,
And thus I'll take my pilgrimage."

D. B. A.

O GOD, Who art to be found by those who truly seek Thee, known by those who love, seen by those whose heart is pure; Thy Spirit possesses all things, speaks in the holy dawn, calls in the quiet even, broods on the deep, and dwells in the heart of man.

Forgive us if we, made to commune with Thee, whose lives were ordered to walk with Thee, have grown insensible to Thy presence, have rested in the things that appear, grown careless of the eternal and the holy. Send now some word of Thine to make a highway to our hearts, and Thyself draw near. Shut us in gathered here, in with Thyself, alone, until every heart burns and each spirit moves toward Thee. May the Spirit of Jesus come upon us and make us at home with Thee. AMEN.

W. E. ORCHARD in *The Temple*

AND I have felt
A presence that disturbs me with the joy
Of elevated thoughts; a sense sublime,
Of something far more deeply interfused,
Whose dwelling is the light of setting suns,
And the round ocean and the living air,

And the blue sky, and in the mind of man;
A motion and a spirit, that impels
All thinking things, all objects of all thought,
And rolls through all things.

WILLIAM WORDSWORTH (1770–1850)
Lines Composed a Few Miles above Tintern Abbey

Nous ne vivons qu'à proportion que nous prions.

JEAN HAMON (1618–1687)

IN one salutation to Thee, my God, let all my senses spread out and touch this world at Thy feet.

Like a rain-cloud of July hung low with its burden of unshed showers let all my mind bend down at Thy door in one salutation to Thee.

Let all my songs gather together their diverse strains into a single current and flow to a sea of silence in one salutation to Thee.

Like a flock of homesick cranes flying night and day back to their mountain nests let all my life take its voyage to its eternal home in one salutation to Thee.

SIR RABINDRANATH TAGORE *Gitanjali*

IN Thee would we lose ourselves utterly; do in us what Thou wilt.

JAKOB BOEHME (1575–1624)

Jakob Boehme was a German who said that he had "seen" into the nature of God, that he himself was his own book whence he learned the truth, that nature rises out of God, and that we, to know ourselves, must sink into Him.

Meditation

ALMIGHTY Father, Source of all blessings, we thank Thee for the preservation of our life and for the joy of living, for the powers of mind and heart and for the wisdom that comes to us from seers and sages filled with Thy spirit.

Teach us to use wisely the blessings Thou hast bestowed upon us. May prosperity not enfeeble our spirit nor harden our heart. May it never so master us as to dull our desire for life's higher ideals.

And should adversity come, may it not embitter us nor cause us to despair, but may we accept it as a mark of Thy chastening love which purifies and strengthens. Let every obstacle become an incentive to greater effort, and let every defeat teach us anew the lesson of patience and perseverance.

Gird us with strength to bear our trials with courage. Let not the loss of anything, however dear to our hearts or precious in our sight, rob us of our faith in Thee. In light as in darkness, in joy as in sorrow, help us to put our trust in Thy providence, that even through our tears we may discern Thy divine blessing. AMEN.

(*Union Prayer Book*)

O CARE unsleeping, Love unchanging, Light unfading; in Thee is all our strength and hope. If Thou didst think no more of us when we thought no more of Thee, how soon we should perish. If Thy love depended on our loveliness, we could hope nothing from Thee. If Thy love was gloomed by our unfaithfulness, how swift and irrevocable our night would be.

Thou art so near us, yet we miss Thee, and often think Thee far away. The path runs straight enough to Thee, yet we lose our way. The knowledge of Thee is clear in us all, yet we are uncertain, and so easily deceived. Thy truth is so simple, and yet it is too hard for us.

We turn to Thee because our feeling of discontent, our sense of sin, our restlessness witness that Thou hast not left us. We silence our thoughts to feel Thee, we hold our eyes to watch for Thee.

Come, as noiseless as the light, and steal within. Brood upon the deep with peace and calm. Touch us with Thy hand that we may turn and see Thy face. AMEN.

W. E. ORCHARD in *The Temple*

Psalm 23

THE Lord is my shepherd; I shall not want.

He maketh me to lie down in green pastures: he leadeth me beside the still waters.

He restoreth my soul: he leadeth me in the paths of righteousness for his name's sake.

Yea, though I walk through the valley of the shadow of death, I will fear no evil: for thou art with me; thy rod and thy staff they comfort me.

Thou preparest a table before me in the presence of mine enemies: thou annointest my head with oil; my cup runneth over.

Surely goodness and mercy shall follow me all the days of my life: and I will dwell in the house of the Lord for ever.

O GOD, in whom we live and move and have our being, enable us to feel the strength that surrounds us, to follow the light that indwells us, and to avail ourselves of the wisdom Thou givest liberally to all who ask of Thee.

Give to us so great a love of truth that we may pass beyond all doubt and error, until our minds are stayed on Thee, and our thoughts are kept in perfect peace.

Give us wisdom to follow the promptings of duty in our daily lives, that we may grow conscious of Thy presence who workest hitherto, and callest us to be fellow-workers now with Thee.

Grant unto us the grace of penitence that we may not grow insensible to our need of forgiveness, from one another, and from Thee; but seek cleansing in communion, fellowship in the light, and rest upon Thy heart. AMEN.

W. E. ORCHARD in *The Temple*

For Pure Thoughts and Intentions

ALMIGHTY God, unto whom all hearts be open, all desires known, and from whom no secrets are hid; Cleanse the thoughts of our hearts by the inspiration of thy holy Spirit, that we may perfectly love thee, and worthily magnify thy holy Name; through Christ our Lord. AMEN.

BISHOP LEOFRIC (1050) *The Book of Common Prayer*

DAY after day, O lord of my life, shall I stand before Thee face to face? With folded hands, O lord of all worlds, shall I stand before Thee face to face?

Under Thy great sky in solitude and silence, with humble heart shall I stand before Thee face to face?

In this laborious world of thine, tumultuous with toil and with struggle, among hurrying crowds shall I stand before Thee face to face?

And when my work shall be done in this world, O King of kings, alone and speechless shall I stand before Thee face to face?

SIR RABINDRANATH TAGORE *Gitanjali*

An Early Greek Prayer

MAY I be no man's enemy, and may I be the friend of that which is eternal and abides. May I never quarrel with those nearest me; and if I do, may I be reconciled quickly. May I never devise evil against any man; if any devise evil against me, may I escape uninjured and without the need of hurting him. May I love, seek, and attain only that which is good. May I wish for all men's happiness and envy none. May I never rejoice in the ill-fortune of one who has wronged me. When I have done or said what is wrong, may I never wait for the rebuke of others, but always rebuke myself until I make amends. . . . May I win no victory that harms either me or my opponent. . . . May I reconcile friends who are wroth with one another. May I, to the extent of my power, give all needful help to my friends and to all who are in want. May I never fail a friend in danger. When visiting those in grief may I be able by gentle and healing words to soften their pain. . . . May I respect myself. . . . May I always keep tame that which rages within me. . . . May I accustom myself to be gentle, and never be angry with people because of circumstances. May I never discuss who is wicked and what wicked things he has done, but know good men and follow in their footsteps.

Attributed to EUSEBIUS, BISHOP OF CÆSAREA (260?–340?) Translated by GILBERT MURRAY.

Of this prayer Gilbert Murray says: "How unpretending is this prayer and yet how searching! And in the whole there is no petition for any material blessing, and—most striking of all—it is addressed to no personal God. It is pure prayer. No one man's attitude towards the Uncharted can be quite the same as his neighbour's. . . . The son shrugs his shoulders at the watchwords that thrilled his father . . . and writes out for himself the manuscript of his creed. Yet, even for the wildest or bravest rebel, that manuscript is only a palimpsest. On the surface all is new writing, clean and self-assertive. Underneath, dim but indelible in the very fibres of the parchment, lie the characters of many ancient aspirations and raptures and battles which his conscious mind has rejected or utterly forgotten. And forgotten things, if there be real life in them, will sometimes return out of the dust, vivid to help still in the forward groping of humanity." (*City without Walls*, p. 749)

A *Prayer*

I HAVE been little used to frame
   Wishes to speech and call it prayer;
To-day, my Father, in thy name,
   I ask to have my soul stript bare
Of all its vain pretense,—to see
   Myself, as I am seen by thee.

I want to know how much the pain
   And passion here, its powers abate;
To take its thoughts, a tangled skein,
   And stretch them out all smooth and straight;
To track its wavering course through sin
   And sorrow, to its origin.

I want to know if in the night
   Of evil, grace doth so abound,
That from its darkness we draw light,
   As flowers do beauty from the ground.
Or, if the sins of time shall be
   The shadows of eternity.

I want, though only for an hour,
   To be myself,—to get more near
The wondrous mystery and power

Of love, whose echoes floating here,
Between us and the waiting grave,
Make all of light, of heaven, we have.

ALICE CARY

Prayer for Stillness

MOST blessed Lord, in Whom is no variableness, neither shadow of turning, Whose stillness is around and within us; to repose in the recollections of Whose Presence is sweetest joy and refreshment, enfold us in this ineffable peace which is Thine own unchanging Will. Still our irritation, soothe our restlessness; say to our hearts, "Peace, be still." Brood over us, within us, Spirit of Perfect Peace, so that outwardly we may reflect the inner stillness of our souls and that we may bear change, distraction, sudden assaults of temptation and disappointments and still be found lying in Thy Heart, O Jesu, enfolded in Thy loving care. Let us be undisturbed, and in true quietness fulfill the calling which is set before us. Be it even so, dear Lord. AMEN. (*Source unverified*)

LIKE summer seas that lave with silent tides a lonely shore, like whispering winds that stir the tops of forest trees, like a still small voice that calls us in the watches of the night, like a child's hand that feels about a fast-closed door; gentle, unnoticed, and oft in vain; so is Thy coming unto us, O God.

Like ships storm-driven into port, like starving souls that seek the bread they once despised, like wanderers begging refuge from the whelming night, like prodigals that seek the father's home when all is spent; yet welcomed at the open door, arms outstretched and kisses for our shame; so is our coming unto Thee, O God.

Like flowers uplifted to the sun, like trees that bend before the storm, like sleeping seas that mirror cloudless skies, like a harp to the hand, like an echo to a cry, like a song to the heart; for all our stubbornness, our failure and our sin; so would we have been to Thee, O God. AMEN.

W. E. ORCHARD in *The Temple*

LET me be quiet now, and kneel,
Who never knelt before,
Here, where the leaves paint patterns light
On a leaf-strewn forest floor;
For I, who saw no God at all
In sea or earth or air,
Baptized by Beauty, now look up
To see God everywhere.

ELLEN FRANCIS GILBERT

For Christ-Likeness

O LORD Jesus, acknowledge what is thine in us, and take away from us all that is not thine; for thy honour and glory. AMEN.

ST. BERNARDINE (1380)

THIS is my prayer to Thee, my lord—strike, strike at the root of penury in my heart.

Give me the strength lightly to bear my joys and sorrows.

Give me the strength to make my love fruitful in service.

Give me the strength never to disown the poor or bend my knees before insolent might.

Give me the strength to raise my mind high above daily trifles.

And give me the strength to surrender my strength to Thy will with love.

SIR RABINDRANATH TAGORE *Gitanjali*

Psalm 139

(In Part)

O LORD, thou hast searched me, and known me.

Thou knowest my downsitting and mine uprising, thou understandest my thought afar off.

Thou compassest my path and my lying down, and art acquainted with all my ways.

For there is not a word in my tongue, but, lo, O Lord, thou knowest it altogether.

Thou hast beset me behind and before, and laid thine hand upon me.

Such knowledge is too wonderful for me; it is high, I cannot attain unto it.

Whither shall I go from thy spirit? or whither shall I flee from thy presence?

If I ascend up into heaven, thou art there: if I make my bed in hell, behold, thou art there.

If I take the wings of the morning, and dwell in the uttermost parts of the sea;

Even there shall thy hand lead me, and thy right hand shall hold me.

If I say, Surely the darkness shall cover me; even the night shall be light about me.

Yea, the darkness hideth not from thee; but the night shineth as the day: the darkness and the light are both alike to thee.

How precious also are thy thoughts unto me, O God! how great is the sum of them!

Search me, O God, and know my heart: try me, and know my thoughts:

And see if there be any wicked way in me, and lead me in the way everlasting.

O GOD, Who hast formed all hearts to love Thee, made all ways to lead to Thy face, created all desire to be unsatisfied save in Thee; with great compassion look upon us gathered here. Our presence is our prayer, our need the only plea we dare to claim, Thy purposes the one assurance we possess.

Some of us are very confused; we do not know why we were ever born, for what end we should live, which way we should take. But we are willing to be guided. Take our trembling hands in Thine, and lead us on.

Some of us are sore within. We long for love and friendship, but we care for no one and we feel that no one cares for us. We are misunderstood, we are lonely, we have been disappointed, we have lost faith in man and our faith in life. Wilt Thou not let us love Thee Who first loved us?

Some of us are vexed with passions that affright us; to yield to them would mean disaster, to restrain them is beyond our power, and nothing earth contains exhausts their vehemence or satisfies their fierce desire.

And so because there is no answer, no end or satisfaction in ourselves; and because we are what we are, and yet long to be so different; we believe Thou art, and that Thou dost understand us. By faith we feel after Thee, through love we find the way, in hope we bring ourselves to Thee. AMEN.

W. E. ORCHARD in *The Temple*

LIFE of my life, I shall ever try to keep my body pure, knowing that Thy living touch is upon all my limbs.

I shall ever try to keep all untruths out from my thoughts, knowing that Thou art that truth which has kindled the light of reason in my mind.

I shall ever try to drive all evils away from my heart and keep my love in flower, knowing that Thou hast Thy seat in the inmost shrine of my heart.

And it shall be my endeavour to reveal Thee in my actions, knowing it is thy power gives me strength to act.

SIR RABINDRANATH TAGORE *Gitanjali*

A *Prayer*

TEACH me, Father, how to go
Softly as the grasses grow;
Hush my soul to meet the shock
Of the wild world as a rock;
But my spirit propt with power,
Make as simple as a flower;
Let the dry heart fill its cup,
Like a poppy looking up,
Let Life lightly wear her crown,
Like the poppy looking down,
When its heart is filled with dew
And its life begins anew.

Teach me, Father, how to be
Kind and patient as a tree;
Joyfully the crickets croon
Under shady oak at noon;
Beetle on his mission bent,
Tarries in that cooling tent;
Let me, also, cheer a spot,
Hidden field or garden grot—
Place where passing souls can rest
On the way and be their best.

EDWIN MARKHAM (1852–1940)

O MOST Merciful, Whose love to us is mighty, long-suffering, and infinitely tender; lead us beyond all idols and imaginations of our minds to contact with Thee the real and abiding; past all barriers of fear and beyond all paralysis of failure to that furnace of flaming purity where falsehood, sin and cowardice are all consumed away. It may be that we know not what we ask; yet we dare not ask for less.

Our aspirations are hindered because we do not know ourselves. We have tried to slake our burning thirst at broken cisterns, to comfort the crying of our spirits with baubles and trinkets, to assuage the pain of our deep unrest by drugging an accusing conscience, believing a lie, and veiling the naked flame that burns within. But now we know Thou makest us never to be content with aught save Thyself, in earth, or heaven, or hell.

Sometimes we have sought Thee in agony and tears, scanned the clouds and watched the ways of men, considered the stars and studied the moral law; and returned from all our search no surer and no nearer. Yet now we know that the impulse to seek Thee came from Thyself alone, and what we sought for was the image Thou hadst first planted in our hearts.

We may not yet hold Thee fast or feel Thee near, but we know Thou holdest us, and all is well. AMEN.

W. E. ORCHARD in *The Temple*

O LORD most high and wonderful, to Whose mind the past and the future meet in our eternal now, to Whose sight all things lie naked and open; we are the creatures of shifting time to whom the past is soon forgotten and from whom the future is completely veiled.

Our day is but a gleam of light between two nights of dark. The mists hang about our minds. Yet we can conceive a higher knowledge beside which ours is poor and incomplete. We are more than we seem, and Thou art nearer than we dream. Yet we only dare to ask for light upon one step ahead, faith to take one day at a time, endurance to wait for the dawn.

Forgive the crushing care that comes from our lack of vision, our fears that the truth will never be clear, our frenzied, ineffectual strivings. Let us feel through all that Thou dost lead us on. Forgive the impertinence that would hurry on the dawn, that would thrust impious hands across the pattern Thou art weaving, that would outrun Thy perfect will for us.

May we become heirs to the Spirit of Jesus, calm because there are twelve hours in the day, confident that the truth shall yet be proclaimed from the housetops, and ever willing to commit ourselves into Thy hands. AMEN.

W. E. ORCHARD in *The Temple*

Crossing the Bar

SUNSET and evening star,
And one clear call for me!
And may there be no moaning of the bar
When I put out to sea.

But such a tide as moving seems asleep
Too full for sound and foam,
When that which drew from out the boundless deep
Turns again home.

Twilight and evening bell
And after that the dark,
And may there be no sadness of farewell
When I embark.

For though from out our bourne of time and place
The flood may bear me far,
I hope to meet my Pilot face to face
When I have crossed the bar.

ALFRED, LORD TENNYSON (1809–1892)

TIME is endless in Thy hands, my lord. There is none to count Thy minutes.

Days and nights pass and ages bloom and fade like flowers. Thou knowest how to wait.

Thy centuries follow each other perfecting a small wild flower.

We have no time to lose, and having no time we must scramble for our chances. We are too poor to be late.

And thus it is that time goes by while I give it to every querulous man who claims it, and Thine altar is empty of all offerings to the last.

At the end of the day I hasten in fear lest Thy gate be shut; but I find that yet there is time.

SIR RABINDRANATH TAGORE *Gitanjali*

II. "OUR ROCK, OUR FORTRESS AND OUR MIGHT"

Faith and Trust

II. "OUR ROCK, OUR FORTRESS AND OUR MIGHT"

FAITH AND TRUST

THE eternal God is thy dwelling place, and underneath are the everlasting arms.

(*Deuteronomy* 33:27)

TO trust is not to fight alone. It is to let God work with you. A man falls overboard. He begins frantically to beat about in the water. He can exhaust his strength in five minutes and go down. If he has learned to float, he can keep up for hours. The depths will sustain him. "Underneath are the everlasting arms." Such support is found through trust, and trust in that spirit which touched the world through Christ is to win not one's own way, or the world's success, but a joy no man can take from us. It is to pass through things temporal so as not to lose the things eternal. The Source of this support, if met in its own spirit, will never let one down.

D. B. A.

"*LORD, I believe; help Thou my unbelief.*"

(*Mark* 9:24)

A Prayer for Trust

LORD, we would learn to trust in Thee at all times. We think we are trusting Thee when the sunlight falls unbroken and bright upon our way; but when the clouds gather and the storm breaks, our hearts faint and our faith loses its vision. May we have such faith as will feel Thee in the dark and walk calmly through the storm. We would learn when we are weary and fretful or tempted and discouraged to be still and know that Thou art God. May we cease our struggling and worrying and let Thee have Thy way with us until around our restlessness flows Thy rest. But may such rest renew our vigor that we may fight the good fight of faith and win the victory; through Jesus Christ our Lord. AMEN.

(*Prayers for Faith and Trust*, compiled
by EDMUND S. ROUSMANIERE)

O LOVE that will not let me go,
I rest my weary soul in thee;
I give thee back the life I owe,
That in thine ocean depths its flow
May richer, fuller, be.

O Light that followest all my way,
I yield my flickering torch to thee;
My heart restores its borrowed ray,
That in thy sunshine's blaze its day
May brighter, fairer, be.

O Joy that seekest me through pain,
I cannot close my heart to thee;
I trace the rainbow through the rain,
And feel the promise is not vain
That morn shall tearless be.

"OUR ROCK, OUR FORTRESS AND OUR MIGHT"

O Cross that liftest up my head,
I dare not ask to fly from thee;
I lay in dust life's glory dead,
And from the ground there blossoms red
Life that shall endless be.

GEORGE MATHESON (1882)

Psalm 46

GOD is our refuge and strength, a very present help in trouble.

Therefore will not we fear, though the earth be removed, and though the mountains be carried into the midst of the sea;

Though the waters thereof roar and be troubled, though the mountains shake with the swelling thereof. Selah.

There is a river, the streams whereof shall make glad the city of God, the holy place of the tabernacles of the most High.

God is in the midst of her; she shall not be moved: God shall help her, and that right early.

The heathen raged, the kingdoms were moved: he uttered his voice, the earth melted.

The Lord of hosts is with us; the God of Jacob is our refuge. Selah.

Come, behold the works of the Lord, what desolations he hath made in the earth.

He maketh wars to cease unto the end of the earth; he breaketh the bow, and cutteth the spear in sunder; he burneth the chariot in the fire.

Be still, and know that I am God: I will be exalted among the heathen, I will be exalted in the earth.

The Lord of hosts is with us; the God of Jacob is our refuge. Selah.

Prayer

MY sorrow had pierced me through; it throbbed in my heart
like a thorn;
This way and that I stared, as a bird with a broken limb
Hearing the hounds' strong feet thrust imminent through the
corn,
So to my God I turned: and I had forgotten Him.

Into the night I breathed a prayer like a soaring fire;
So to the windswept cliff the resonant rocket streams,
And it struck its mark, I know; for I felt my flying desire
Strain, like a rope drawn home, and catch in the land of dreams.

What was the answer? *This*—the horrible depth of night,
And deeper, as ever I peer, the huge cliff's mountainous shade,
While the frail boat cracks and grinds, and never a star in sight,
And the seething waves smite fiercer—*and yet I am not afraid.*

ARTHUR CHRISTOPHER BENSON

Confidence in God's Providence

GRANT unto us, Almighty God, the peace of God that passeth understanding, that we, amid the storms and troubles of this our life, may rest in Thee, knowing that all things are in Thee; not beneath Thine eye only, but under Thy care, governed by Thy will, guarded by Thy love, so that with a quiet heart we may see the storms of life, the cloud and the thick darkness, ever rejoicing to know that the darkness and the light are both alike to Thee. Guide, guard, and govern us even to the end, that none of us may fail to lay hold upon the immortal life; through Jesus Christ our Lord. AMEN.

GEORGE DAWSON (1821–1876)

The Prayer of Lady Jane Grey in Her Last Imprisonment

O MERCIFUL God, be Thou unto me a strong tower of defence, I humbly entreat Thee. Give me grace to await Thy leisure, and patiently to bear what Thou doest unto me; nothing doubting or mistrusting Thy goodness towards me; for Thou knowest what is good for me better than I do. Therefore do with me in all things what Thou wilt; only arm me, I beseech Thee, with Thine armour, that I may stand fast; above all things, taking to me the shield of faith; praying always that I may refer myself wholly to Thy will, abiding Thy pleasure, and comforting myself in those troubles which it shall please Thee to send me, seeing such troubles are profitable for me; and I am assuredly persuaded that all Thou doest cannot but be well; and unto Thee be all honour and glory. AMEN.

LADY JANE GREY (1537–1554)

This brilliant and noble woman was the innocent victim of plots to seize the throne of England. She was the great-granddaughter of Henry VII and the wife of the Earl of Dudley. Proclaimed Queen in 1553, she was deposed a few months later and executed with her husband on Tower Hill the following year.

For Perfect Trust in God

O LORD, our heavenly Father, Who orderest all things for our eternal good, mercifully enlighten our minds, and give us a firm and abiding trust in Thy love and care. Silence our murmurings, quiet our fears, and dispel our doubts, that, rising above our afflictions and our anxieties, we may rest on Thee, the Rock of everlasting Strength; through Jesus Christ our Lord. AMEN.

New Church Book of Worship, 1876

Psalm 27

THE Lord is my light and my salvation; whom shall I fear? the Lord is the strength of my life; of whom shall I be afraid?

When the wicked, even mine enemies and my foes, came upon me to eat up my flesh, they stumbled and fell.

Though an host should encamp against me, my heart shall not fear: though war should rise against me, in this will I be confident.

One thing have I desired of the Lord, that will I seek after; that I may dwell in the house of the Lord all the days of my life, to behold the beauty of the Lord, and to enquire in his temple.

For in the time of trouble he shall hide me in his pavilion: in the secret of his tabernacle shall he hide me; he shall set me up upon a rock.

And now shall mine head be lifted up above mine enemies round about me: therefore will I offer in his tabernacle sacrifices of joy; I will sing, yea, I will sing praises unto the Lord.

Hear, O Lord, when I cry with my voice: have mercy also upon me, and answer me.

When thou saidst, Seek ye my face; my heart said unto thee, Thy face, Lord, will I seek.

Hide not thy face far from me; put not thy servant away in anger: thou hast been my help; leave me not, neither forsake me, O God of my salvation.

When my father and my mother forsake me, then the Lord will take me up.

Teach me thy way, O Lord, and lead me in a plain path, because of mine enemies.

Deliver me not over unto the will of mine enemies: for false witnesses are risen up against me, and such as breathe out cruelty.

I had fainted, unless I believed to see the goodness of the Lord in the land of the living.

Wait on the Lord: be of good courage, and he shall strengthen thine heart: wait, I say, on the Lord.

O GOD, our help in ages past,
  Our hope for years to come,
Our shelter from the stormy blast
  And our eternal home:

Under the shadow of Thy throne
  Thy saints have dwelt secure;
Sufficient is Thine arm alone,
  And our defense is sure.

Before the hills in order stood,
  Or earth received her frame,
From everlasting Thou art God,
  To endless years the same.

A thousand ages in Thy sight
  Are like an evening gone;
Short as the watch that ends the night
  Before the rising sun.

Time, like an ever-rolling stream,
  Bears all its sons away;
They fly, forgotten, as a dream
  Dies at the opening day.

O God, our help in ages past,
  Our hope for years to come,
Be Thou our guide while life shall last,
  And our eternal home.

SIR ISAAC WATTS (1674–1748)

Although a scholar and theologian of high attainments, Isaac Watts preferred parish life; and although an all-round master of his profession, music and hymn writing were his passion. He was practically the first to break through the limitation of singing to metrical Psalms and to introduce the early modern hymn.

O LORD, Thou knowest what is best for us, let this or that be done, as Thou shalt please. Give what Thou wilt, and how much Thou wilt, and when Thou wilt. Deal with me as Thou thinkest good, and as best pleaseth Thee. Set me where Thou wilt, and deal with me in all things just as Thou wilt. Behold, I am Thy servant, prepared for all things; for I desire not to live unto myself, but unto Thee; and Oh, that I could do it worthily and perfectly! AMEN.

THOMAS À KEMPIS (1380–1471)

The reputed author of The Imitation of Christ, *possibly the most widely popular pre-Reformation devotional book, possibly also, by encouraging direct communion with God, one of the contributing causes of the Reformation.*

Prayer from "In Memoriam"

STRONG Son of God, immortal Love,
  Whom we that have not seen thy face,
  By faith, and faith alone, embrace,
Believing where we cannot prove;

Thine are these orbs of light and shade;
  Thou madest Life in man and brute;
  Thou madest Death; and lo, thy foot
Is on the skull which thou hast made.

Thou wilt not leave us in the dust;
  The highest, holiest manhood, thou;
  Our wills are ours, we know not how;
Our wills are ours, to make them thine.

Our little systems have their day;
They have their day and cease to be;
They are but broken lights of thee,
And thou, O Lord, art more than they. . . .

Forgive these wild and wandering cries,
Confusions of a wasted youth;
Forgive them where they fail in truth,
And in thy wisdom make me wise.

ALFRED, LORD TENNYSON (1809–1892)

For Quiet Confidence

O GOD of Peace, Who hast taught us that in returning and rest we shall be saved, in quietness and in confidence shall be our strength; By the might of Thy Spirit lift us, we pray Thee, to Thy presence, where we may be still and know that Thou art God; through Jesus Christ our Lord. AMEN.

(*War-Time Prayers*)

For Confidence in God

ALMIGHTY God, Lord of the storm and of the calm, the vexed sea and the quiet haven, of day and night, of life and of death; grant unto us so to have our hearts stayed upon Thy faithfulness, Thine unchangingness and love, that, whatsoever betide us, however black the cloud or dark the night, with quiet faith trusting in Thee, we may look upon Thee with untroubled eye, and walking in lowliness towards Thee, and in lovingness towards one another, abide all storms and troubles of this mortal life, beseeching Thee that they may turn to the soul's true good; we ask it for Thy mercy's sake, shown in Jesus Christ our Lord. AMEN.

GEORGE DAWSON (1821–1876)

LORD of all being; throned afar,
Thy glory flames from sun and star;
Centre and soul of every sphere,
Yet to each loving heart how near!

Sun of our life, Thy quickening ray
Sheds on our path the glow of day;
Star of our hope, Thy softened light
Cheers the long watches of the night.

Our midnight is Thy smile withdrawn;
Our noontide is Thy gracious dawn;
Our rainbow arch, Thy mercy's sign;
All, save the clouds of sin, are Thine.

Lord of all life, below, above,
Whose light is truth, Whose warmth is love,
Before Thy ever-blazing throne
We ask no lustre of our own.

Grant us Thy truth to make us free,
And kindling hearts that burn for Thee,
Till all Thy living altars claim
One holy light, one heavenly flame.

OLIVER WENDELL HOLMES
(1809–1894)

O LORD, Thou knowest what is the better way, let this or that be done as Thou shalt please. Give what Thou wilt, and how much Thou wilt, and when Thou wilt. Deal with me as Thou knowest, and best pleaseth Thee, and is most for Thy honor. Set me where Thou wilt, and deal with me in all things as Thou wilt. I am in Thy hand; turn me round and turn me back again, even as a wheel. Behold I am Thy servant, prepared for all things; for I desire not to live unto myself, but unto Thee; and Oh that I could do it worthily and perfectly!

THOMAS À KEMPIS (1380–1471)

Lord Nelson's Prayer

MAY the Great God, whom I worship, grant to my country and for the benefit of Europe in general, a great and glorious victory, and may no misconduct in any one tarnish it; and may humanity after victory be the predominant feature in the British fleet! For myself individually, I commit my life to Him that made me; and may His blessing alight on my endeavors for serving my country faithfully! To Him I resign myself, and the just cause which is entrusted to me to defend.

AMEN! AMEN! AMEN!

HORATIO, LORD NELSON (1758–1805)

On the morning of October 21, 1803, before the Battle of Trafalgar Nelson gave a signal to bear down on the enemy in two lines. Southey says: "Having seen that all was as it should be, Nelson retired to his cabin and wrote the . . . prayer." (SOUTHEY, Life of Nelson)

O LORD my God, I have trusted in thee;
O Jesu my dearest one, now set me free.
In prison's oppression, in sorrow's obsession,
I weary for thee.
With sighing and crying bowed down as dying,
I adore thee, I implore thee, set me free!
(O Domine Deus! speravi in te;
O care mi Jesu! nunc libera me.
In dura catena, in misera poëna,
Desidero te.

Languendo, jemendo, et genuflectendo,
Adoro, imploro, ut liberes me!)

MARY, QUEEN OF SCOTS (1542–1587)

Written in her Book of Devotions before her execution. (SWINBURNE, Mary Stewart, *Act V, sc.* 1)

Dost Thou Not Care?

I LOVE and love not; Lord it breaks my heart
To love and not to love.
Thus veiled within thy glory, gone apart
Into thy shrine, which is above.
Dost thou not love me, Lord, or care
For this mine ill?
I love thee here or there,
I will accept thy broken heart; lie still.

Lord it was well with me in time gone by,
That cometh not again,
When I was fresh and cheerful; worn with pain
Now, out of sight and out of heart;
O, Lord, how long?
I watch thee as thou art
I will accept thy fainting heart; be strong.

"Lie still," "be strong," to-day; but, Lord, to-morrow,
What of to-morrow, Lord?
Shall there be rest from toil, be truce from sorrow,
Be living green upon the sward
Now but a barren grave to me,
Be joy or sorrow?
Did I not die for thee?
Do I not live for thee? Leave me to-morrow.

CHRISTINA G. ROSSETTI (1830–1894)

MY faith looks up to thee,
Thou Lamb of Calvary,
Saviour divine!
Now hear me while I pray;
Take all my guilt away;
O let me from this day
Be wholly thine.

May thy rich grace impart
Strength to my fainting heart,
My zeal inspire;
As thou hast died for me,
O may my love to thee
Pure, warm, and changeless be,
A living fire.

While life's dark maze I tread,
And griefs around me spread,
Be thou my guide;
Bid darkness turn to day;
Wipe sorrow's tears away;
Nor let me ever stray
From thee aside!

When ends life's transient dream,
When death's cold, sullen stream
Shall o'er me roll;
Blest Saviour, then in love,
Fear and distrust remove;
O bear me safe above,
A ransomed soul! AMEN.

RAY PALMER

“OUR ROCK, OUR FORTRESS AND OUR MIGHT”

Tant que je respire, j’espere.

JOHN CALVIN (1509–1564)

Last Lines

NO coward soul is mine,
No trembler in the world’s storm-troubled sphere:
I see heaven’s glories shine,
And faith shines equal, arming me from fear.

O God within my breast,
Almighty, ever-present Deity!
Life—that in me has rest,
As I—undying life—have power in Thee!

Vain are the thousand creeds
That move men’s hearts:
Unutterably vain; worthless as withered reeds,
Or idlest froth amid the boundless main,

To waken doubt in one
Holding so fast by thine infinity;
So surely anchor’d on
The steadfast rock of immortality.

With wide-embracing love
Thy Spirit animates eternal years,
Pervades and broods above,
Changes, sustains, dissolves, creates, and rears.

Though earth and man were gone,
And suns and universes ceased to be,
And Thou wert left alone,
Every existence would exist in Thee.

There is not room for Death,
 Nor atom that his might could render void:
Thou—*Thou* art Being and Breath,
 And what *Thou* art may never be destroy'd.

EMILY BRONTË (1818–1848)

There is no more interesting or pathetic story in English literature than that of the Brontë sisters, Charlotte and Emily. Their girlhood was buried in a dreary Yorkshire parsonage, yet almost simultaneously they sprang to fame as novelists by the publication of Jane Eyre *and* Wuthering Heights. *Emily Brontë achieved a high place with her verse as well. These "Last Lines" have been characterized as "the finest achievement in poetry that any woman has given to English literature."*

At Last

WHEN on my day of life the night is falling,
 And, in the winds from unsunned spaces blown,
I hear far voices out of darkness calling
 My feet to paths unknown,

Thou who hast made my home of life so pleasant,
 Leave not its tenant when its walls decay;
O Love Divine, O Helper ever-present,
 Be Thou my strength and stay!

Be near me when all else is from me drifting;
 Earth, sky, home's pictures, days of shade and shine,
And kindly faces to my own uplifting
 The love which answers mine.

I have but Thee, my Father! let Thy spirit
 Be with me then to comfort and uphold;
No gate of pearl, no branch of palm I merit,
 Nor street of shining gold.

"OUR ROCK, OUR FORTRESS AND OUR MIGHT"

Suffice it if—my good and ill unreckoned,
And both forgiven through Thy unbounding grace—
I find myself by hands familiar beckoned
Unto my fitting place.

JOHN GREENLEAF WHITTIER
(1807–1892)

III. CALM AFTER STORM

Penitence and Pardon

III. CALM AFTER STORM

PENITENCE AND PARDON

"IN His will is our peace."

DANTE

THE lives of the Saints are a record of sin! In their human weaknesses lay their strength, because they faced them and acknowledged them and let something Other supplant them. Two things cannot stand in the same place at the same time. A law of the spiritual life makes the same assertion: "Whatsoever things are honest, whatsoever things are just, whatsoever things are lovely, whatsoever things are of good report; if there be any virtue, and if there be any praise, think on these things."

Where conscience inspires genuine contrition and registers honest regret, God gives release. Penitence and pardon are as established in their sequence as darkness and dawn, provided one honestly wants to fashion a new day.

"Love God, and you can do as you please," said St. Augustine.

D. B. A.

TWO men went up into the temple to pray; the one a Pharisee, and the other a publican.

The Pharisee stood and prayed thus with himself, God, I thank thee, that I am not as other men are, extortioners, unjust, adulterers, or even as this publican.

I fast twice in the week, I give tithes of all that I possess.

And the publican, standing afar off, would not lift up so much as his eyes unto heaven, but smote upon his breast, saying, God be merciful to me a sinner.

(*Luke* 18:10–13)

ALMIGHTY and most merciful Father; We have erred, and strayed from thy ways like lost sheep. We have followed too much the devices and desires of our own hearts. We have offended against thy holy laws. We have left undone those things which we ought to have done; And we have done those things which we ought not to have done; And there is no health in us. But thou, O Lord, have mercy upon us, miserable offenders. Spare thou those, O God, who confess their faults. Restore thou those who are penitent; According to thy promises declared unto mankind In Christ Jesus our Lord. And grant, O most merciful Father, for his sake; That we may hereafter live a godly, righteous, and sober life, To the glory of thy holy Name. AMEN.

(*The Book of Common Prayer*)

Prayer

O GOD of earth and altar,
Bow down and hear our cry,
Our earthly rulers falter,
Our people drift and die;
The walls of gold entomb us,
The swords of scorn divide,
Take not Thy thunder from us
But take away our pride!

From all that terror teaches,
From lies of tongue and pen,
From all the easy speeches
That comfort cruel men,
From sale and profanation
Of honor and the sword,
From sleep and from damnation
Deliver us, Good Lord!

GILBERT KEITH CHESTERTON
(1874–1936)

For Mercy and Forgiveness

ALMIGHTY and everlasting God, Who art always more ready to hear than we to pray, and art wont to give more than either we desire or deserve, pour down upon us the abundance of Thy mercy, forgiving us those things whereof our conscience is afraid, and giving us those good things which we are not worthy to ask, but through the merits and mediation of Jesus Christ, Thy Son, our Lord. AMEN.

(*Leonine Sacramentary*, 440)

AND now where the justice of God cannot forget, may His everlasting mercy in kindness forgive; for the sake of Jesus Christ our Lord. AMEN.

D. B. A.

Invocation to Ormazd

Persian

IN the name of God, the Giver, Forgiver, rich in love, praise be to the name of Ormazd, the God with the name who always was, always is, and always will be; the heavenly among the heavenly, with the name "From whom alone is derived rule."

With all strength bring I thanks.

All good do I accept at thy command, O God, and think, and speak, and do it. I believe in the pure law; by every good work seek I forgiveness for all sins. I keep pure the six powers—thought, speech, work, memory, mind, and understanding. According to thy will am I able to accomplish, O accomplisher of good, thy honor, with good thoughts, good works. . . .

Praise be to the Overseer, the Lord, who rewards those who accomplish good deeds according to his own wish, and at last purifies even the wicked ones of hell.

(*Pagan Prayers*)

The Fool's Prayer

THE royal feast was done; the king
Sought some new sport to banish care,
And to his jester cried: "Sir Fool,
Kneel now, and make for us a prayer!"

The jester doffed his cap and bells,
And stood the mocking court before;
They could not see the bitter smile
Behind the painted grin he wore.

He bowed his head, and bent his knee
Upon the monarch's silken stool;
His pleading voice arose: "O Lord,
Be merciful to me, a fool!

"No pity, Lord, could change the heart
From red with wrong, to white as wool;
The rod must heal the sin; but, Lord,
Be merciful to me, a fool!

CALM AFTER STORM

" 'Tis not by guilt the onward sweep
Of truth and right, O Lord, we stay;
'Tis by our follies that so long
We hold the earth from heaven away.

"These clumsy feet, still in the mire,
Go crushing blossoms without end;
These hard, well-meaning hands we thrust
Among the heart-strings of a friend.

"The ill-timed truth we might have kept—
Who knows how sharp it pierced and stung!
The word we had not sense to say—
Who knows how grandly it had rung?

"Our faults no tenderness should ask,
The chastening stripes must cleanse them all;
But for our blunders—oh, in shame,
Before the eyes of heaven we fall.

"Earth bears no balsam for mistakes;
Men crown the knave, and scourge the tool
That did his will; but Thou, O Lord,
Be merciful to me, a fool!"

The room was hushed; in silence rose
The King, and sought his gardens cool,
And walked apart, and murmured low,
"Be merciful to me, a fool!"

EDWARD ROWLAND SILL

O LORD, we beseech thee, mercifully hear our prayers, and spare all those who confess their sins unto thee; that they, whose consciences by sin are accused, by thy merciful pardon may be absolved; through Christ our Lord. AMEN.

(*The Book of Common Prayer*)

SAVIOUR! when in dust to Thee
Low we bow the adoring knee,
When, repentant, to the skies
Scarce we lift our weeping eyes,
Oh! by all Thy pains and woe
Suffered once for man below;
Bending from Thy throne on high,
Hear our solemn litany!

By Thy helpless infant years,
By Thy life of want and tears,
By Thy days of sore distress
In the savage wilderness,
By the dread permitted hour
Of the mighty tempter's power:
Turn, oh turn a favoring eye,
Hear our solemn litany!

By the sacred grief that wept
O'er the grave where Lazarus slept;
By the boding tears that flowed
Over Salem's loved abode;
By the anguished sigh that told
Treachery lurked within Thy fold;
From Thy seat above the sky,
Hear our solemn litany!

By the burthen Thou didst bear,
By Thine agony of prayer,
By the cross, the nail, the thorn,
Piercing spear, and torturing scorn;
By the gloom that veiled the skies
O'er the dreadful sacrifice;
Listen to our humble cry,
Hear our solemn litany!

By Thy deep expiring groan;
By the sealed sepulchral stone;
By the vault, whose dark abode
Held in vain the rising God:
Oh! from earth to heaven restored,
Mighty, re-ascended Lord,
Listen, listen to the cry
Of our solemn litany!

ROBERT GRANT (1815)

O GOD, Thou power so patient with us, Thou hast seen us let watching eyes grow dim and waiting hearts grow hard, because we have not cared enough. Turn us about, we beseech Thee, to seek out the lonely heart and the needy life to give it Thy good Spirit of faithful understanding. And where it is too late, do Thou, O God, forgive and mercifully lay it not to our charge. Fill the hours which remain to us; cleanse our eyes that we may see more clearly; open our hearts that we may love more dearly; even as we have been loved; through Jesus Christ our Lord. AMEN.

D. B. A.

Mea Culpa

BE pitiful, my God!
  No hard-won gifts I bring—
But empty, pleading hands
  To Thee at evening.

Spring came, white-browed and young;
  I, too, was young with Spring.
There was a blue, blue heaven
  Above a skylark's wing.

Youth is the time for joy,
  I cried, it is not meet
To mount the heights of toil
  With child-soft feet.

When Summer walked the land
  In Passion's red arrayed,
Under green sweeping boughs,
  My couch I made.

The noon-tide heat was sore,
  I slept the Summer through:
An angel waked me—"Thou
  Hast work to do."

I rose and saw the sheaves
  Upstanding in a row:
The reapers sang Thy praise
  While passing to and fro.

My hands were soft with ease;
Long were the Autumn hours:
I left the ripened sheaves
For poppy-flowers.

But lo! now Winter glooms,
And gray is in my hair;
Whither has flown the world
I found so fair?

My patient God, forgive!
Praying Thy pardon sweet
I lay a lonely heart
Before Thy feet.

ETHNA CARBERRY (*Loyola Book of Verse*)

WE humbly beseech thee, O Father, mercifully to look upon our infirmities; and, for the glory of thy Name, turn from us all those evils that we most justly have deserved; and grant, that in all our troubles we may put our whole trust and confidence in thy mercy, and evermore serve thee in holiness and pureness of living, to thy honour and glory; through our only Mediator and Advocate, Jesus Christ our Lord. AMEN.

(*The Book of Common Prayer*)

"To Be More Than Conquerors Through Him Who Loved Us"

NOW, O God, our Saviour, we entreat Thee, subdue our iniquities. Only Thine Almighty arm can vanquish them. We look to Thee for victory. Fight for us, fight in us, that we may be more than conquerors, through Him who loved us, even Jesus Christ, our only Lord and Saviour. AMEN.

E. BICKERSTETH (1786)

JUST as I am, without one plea,
But that Thy blood was shed for me,
And that Thou bidd'st me come to Thee,
O Lamb of God, I come.

Just as I am, and waiting not
To rid my soul of one dark blot,
To Thee, Whose blood can cleanse each spot,
O Lamb of God, I come.

Just as I am, though tossed about
With many a conflict, many a doubt,
Fightings and fears within, without,
O Lamb of God, I come.

Just as I am, poor, wretched, blind;
Sight, riches, healing of the mind,
Yea, all I need, in Thee to find,
O Lamb of God, I come.

Just as I am: Thou wilt receive,
Wilt welcome, pardon, cleanse, relieve;
Because Thy promise I believe,
O Lamb of God, I come.

Just as I am, Thy love unknown
Has broken every barrier down;
Now to be Thine, yea, Thine alone,
O Lamb of God, I come.

CHARLOTTE ELLIOTT (1836)

Psalm 51

(In Part)

HAVE mercy upon me, O God, according to thy lovingkindness: according unto the multitude of thy tender mercies blot out my transgressions.

Wash me throughly from mine iniquity, and cleanse me from my sin.

For I acknowledge my transgressions: and my sin is ever before me. . . .

Hide thy face from my sins, and blot out all mine iniquities.

Create in me a clean heart, O God; and renew a right spirit within me.

Cast me not away from thy presence; and take not thy holy spirit from me.

Restore unto me the joy of thy salvation; and uphold me with thy free spirit. . . .

For thou desirest not sacrifice; else would I give it: thou delightest not in burnt offering.

The sacrifices of God are a broken spirit: a broken and a contrite heart, O God, thou wilt not despise.

A Hymn to God the Father

Wilt Thou forgive that sin, where I begun,
 Which was my sin, though it were done before?
Wilt Thou forgive that sin through which I run,
 And do run still, though still I do deplore?
When Thou hast done, Thou hast not done,
 For I have more.

Wilt Thou forgive that sin which I have won
  Others to sin, and made my sin their door?
Wilt Thou forgive that sin which I did shun
  A year or two, but wallowed in a score?
When Thou hast done, Thou hast not done,
  For I have more.

I have a sin of fear, that when I've spun
  My last thread, I still perish on the shore;
But swear by Thyself, that at my death Thy Son
  Shall shine, as he shines now and heretofore,
And having done that, Thou hast done;
  I fear no more!

JOHN DONNE (1573–1631)

In youth somewhat of a worldling, always scholarly, John Donne thought himself out of Romanism into Anglicanism, retaining to the end the rich mysticism of both; next to Launcelot Andrewes he was probably the leading religious influence of his day.

O GOD, whose nature and property is ever to have mercy and to forgive; Receive our humble petitions; and though we be tied and bound with the chain of our sins, yet let the pitifulness of thy great mercy loose us; for the honour of Jesus Christ, our Mediator and Advocate. AMEN.

(*The Book of Common Prayer*)

Psalm 130

OUT of the depths have I cried unto thee, O Lord.

Lord, hear my voice: let thine ears be attentive to the voice of my supplications.

If thou, Lord, shouldest mark iniquities, O Lord, who shall stand?

But there is forgiveness with thee, that thou mayest be feared.

I wait for the Lord, my soul doth wait, and in his word do I hope.

My soul waiteth for the Lord more than they that watch for the morning: I say, more than they that watch for the morning.

Let Israel hope in the Lord: for with the Lord there is mercy, and with him is plenteous redemption.

FOUR things which are not in thy treasury,
I lay before thee, Lord, with this petition:—
  My nothingness, my wants,
  My sins, and my contrition.

ROBERT SOUTHEY, (1774–1843)
Occasional Pieces, No. 19

A Last Prayer

FATHER, I scarcely dare to pray,
  So clear I see, now it is done,
That I have wasted half my day,
  And left my work but just begun;

So clear I see that things I thought
  Were right or harmless were a sin;
So clear I see that I have sought
  Unconscious, selfish aims to win;

So clear I see that I have hurt
  The soul I might have helped to save;
That I have slothful been, inert,
  Deaf to the calls thy leaders gave.

In outskirts of thy kingdoms vast,
Father, the humblest spot give me;
Set me the lowliest task thou hast:
Let me repentant work for thee!

HELEN HUNT JACKSON (1830–1885)

Mrs. Jackson was famous for her novel Ramona, *written to illustrate the abominable treatment of the Indians by the whites. The accompanying prayer was composed in her last, lingering illness.*

Prayer of the Thief upon the Cross

"LORD, remember me when thou comest into thy kingdom."

(*Luke* 23:42)

An Evening Prayer

IF I have wounded any soul today,
If I have caused one foot to go astray,
If I have walked in my own willful way—
Good Lord, forgive.

If I have uttered idle words or vain,
If I have turned aside from want or pain
Lest I myself should suffer through the strain—
Good Lord, forgive.

If I have craved for joys that are not mine,
If I have let my wayward heart repine
Dwelling on things on earth, not things divine—
Good Lord, forgive.

CALM AFTER STORM

If I have been perverse, or hard, or cold,
If I have longed for shelter in the fold
When Thou hast given me some part to hold—
Good Lord, forgive.

Forgive the sins I have confessed to Thee,
Forgive the secret sins I do not see;
That which I know not, Father, teach Thou me—
Help me to live.

C. Maude Battersby

IV. FROM THE HEIGHTS

Thanksgiving

IV. FROM THE HEIGHTS

THANKSGIVING

A SINGLE *grateful thought towards heaven is the most complete prayer. . . .*

LESSING, Minna von Barnhelm,
Act II, sc. 7

A THANKFUL heart is always hopeful. To be aware of the beautiful along with the ugly, to be alert to see the good together with the bad, to climb high enough to see the view all around, develops a life with no blind spots. So even in the face of the swiftest blows we are more likely to keep our perspective fairly true. When an impending tragedy, plainly unavoidable, may haunt us, we may only look at what will happen. Or we may regard the intervening days as a chance to make every moment count for a loved one's happiness. We can confidently meet what happens as we thus discover what life can be, learning what life really *is*. The beautiful, the good, are their own best advocates of their everlastingness. To be aware of them and to appreciate them and to thank God for them may not alter what happens, but it does affect the way life looks to us and the way we can stand up to it.

D. B. A.

A General Thanksgiving

ALMIGHTY God, Father of all mercies, we, thine unworthy servants, do give thee most humble and hearty thanks for all thy goodness and loving-kindness to us, and to all men. We bless thee for our creation, preservation, and all the blessings of this life; but above all, for thine inestimable love in the redemption of the world by our Lord Jesus Christ; for the means of grace, and for the hope of glory. And, we beseech thee, give us that due sense of all thy mercies, that our hearts may be unfeignedly thankful; and that we show forth thy praise, not only with our lips, but in our lives, by giving up our selves to thy service, and by walking before thee in holiness and righteousness all our days; through Jesus Christ our Lord, to whom, with thee and the Holy Ghost, be all honour and glory, world without end. AMEN.

(*The Book of Common Prayer*)

THOU hast given so much to us, give one thing more, a grateful heart; for Christ's sake. AMEN.

GEORGE HERBERT (1593–1633)

A friend of scholars, the brother of a scholar, a scholar in his own right, George Herbert left the university for parish life, finding in the government, in the liturgy and in the pastoral work of the English Church complete intellectual and religious freedom.

A Thanksgiving to God, for His House

LORD, thou hast given me a cell,
Wherein to dwell;
A little house, whose humble roof
Is weather proof;

Under the spars of which I lie
　　Both soft and dry;
Where thou, my chamber for to ward,
　　Hast set a guard
Of harmless thoughts, to watch and keep
　　Me, while I sleep.
Low is my porch, as is my fate;
　　Both void of state;
And yet the threshold of my door
　　Is worn by th' poor,
Who hither come and freely get
　　Good words or meat.
Like as my parlor, so my hall
　　And kitchen's small;
A little buttery, and therein
　　A little bin,
Which keeps my little loaf of bread
　　Unchipt, unflead; *
Some brittle sticks of thorn or briar
　　Make me a fire,
Close by whose living coal I sit,
　　And glow like it.
Lord, I confess too, when I dine
　　The pulse is thine,
And all those other bits that be
　　There placed by thee;
The worts, the purslane, and the mess
　　Of water-cress,
Which of thy kindness thou hast sent;
　　And my content
Makes those, and my beloved beet,
　　To be more sweet.
'Tis thou that crown'st my glittering hearth

* Whole.

With guiltless mirth,
And giv'st me wassail bowl to drink,
Spiced to the brink.
Lord, 'tis thy plenty-dropping hand
That soils my land;
And giv'st me, for my bushel sown,
Twice ten for one:
Thou mak'st my teeming hen to lay
Her egg each day;
Besides my healthful ewes to bear
Me twins each year;
The while the conduits of my kine
Run cream (for wine).
That I should render, for my part,
A thankful heart:
Which, fired with incense, I resign,
As wholly Thine;
But the acceptance, that must be,
My Christ, by Thee.

ROBERT HERRICK (1591–1674)

Robert Herrick was a scholar, a wit, a poet, and a parish priest, spending most of his life in the rural parish of Dean Prior in Devonshire, increasing in his understanding of his people and in his affection for them, and, when not writing for sheer amusement, turning into verse his deeper thoughts of men and God.

A Litany of Thanksgiving

ALMIGHTY God, our Heavenly Father, from Whom cometh every good and perfect gift, we call to remembrance Thy loving kindness and Thy tender mercies which have ever been of old, and with grateful hearts we would lift up to Thee the voice of our thanksgiving.

For all the gifts which Thou hast bestowed upon us and our race;
For the life Thou hast given us, and the world in which we live:
For these, Thy gifts
We praise Thee, O God.

For the work we are enabled to do, and
For the truth we are permitted to learn;
For whatever of good there has been in our lives,
For all the hopes and aspirations which lead us onwards to better things:
For these, Thy gifts
We praise Thee, O God.

For the order and constancy of nature;
For the beauty and bounty of the world;
For day and night, summer and winter, seedtime and harvest;
For the varied gifts of loveliness and use which every season brings:
For these, Thy gifts
We praise Thee, O God.

For the Autumn with all its glories;
For the Harvest with its boundless store;
For all the fruits of the earth that gladden and sustain the life of man:
For these, Thy gifts
We praise Thee, O God.

For all the comforts and gladness of life;
For our homes and all our home-blessings;

For our friends and all the pure pleasures of social intercourse:

For these, Thy gifts

We praise Thee, O God.

And most of all and above all:

For the gift of Thy Son Jesus Christ, and all helps and hopes which are ours as His disciples;

For His life and death—His resurrection and ascension for our redemption;

For the presence and inspiration of Thy Holy Spirit and for all the ministries of Thy truth and grace:

We praise Thee, O God.

For communion with Thee, the Father of our spirits;

For the light and peace that are gained through trust and obedience to Thy laws:

We praise Thee, O God.

For all the discipline of life;

For the tasks and trials by which we are trained to patience, self-knowledge and self-conquest;

For all the circumstances which bring us into closer sympathy with our suffering brethren;

For troubles which have lifted us nearer Thee and drawn us into deeper fellowship with Jesus Christ:

We praise Thee, O God.

For the sacred and tender ties which bind us to the unseen world;

For the faith which dispels the shadows of earth, and fills the saddest, and the last moments of life with the light of an immortal hope:

We praise Thee, O God.

God of all grace and love, we have praised Thee with our lips; Grant that we may also praise Thee in consecrated and faithful lives, to Thy honour and glory, through Jesus Christ our Lord. AMEN.

J. HUNTER (Adapted)

Psalm 103

BLESS the Lord, O my soul: and all that is within me, bless his holy name.

Bless the Lord, O my soul, and forget not all his benefits:

Who forgiveth all thine iniquities; who healeth all thy diseases;

Who redeemeth thy life from destruction; who crowneth thee with lovingkindness and tender mercies;

Who satisfieth thy mouth with good things; so that thy youth is renewed like the eagle's.

The Lord executeth righteousness and judgment for all that are oppressed.

He made known his ways unto Moses, his acts unto the children of Israel.

The Lord is merciful and gracious, slow to anger, and plenteous in mercy.

He will not always chide: neither will he keep his anger for ever.

He hath not dealt with us after our sins; nor rewarded us according to our iniquities.

For as the heaven is high above the earth, so great is his mercy toward them that fear him.

As far as the east is from the west, so far hath he removed our transgressions from us.

Like as a father pitieth his children, so the Lord pitieth them that fear him.

For he knoweth our frame; he remembereth that we are dust.

As for man, his days are as grass: as a flower of the field, so he flourisheth.

For the wind passeth over it, and it is gone; and the place thereof shall know it no more.

But the mercy of the Lord is from everlasting to everlasting upon them that fear him, and his righteousness unto children's children;

To such as keep his covenant, and to those that remember his commandments to do them.

The Lord hath prepared his throne in the heavens; and his kingdom ruleth over all.

Bless the Lord, ye his angels, that excel in strength, that do his commandments, hearkening unto the voice of his word.

Bless ye the Lord, all ye his hosts; ye ministers of his, that do his pleasure.

Bless the Lord, all his works in all places of his dominion: bless the Lord, O my soul.

For Joy in God

O GOD, who makest cheerfulness the companion of strength; Grant us so to rejoice in the gift of thy power, that being freed from all fretfulness and despair, we may glorify thee in word and deed; through Jesus Christ our Lord. AMEN.

(*Source unverified*)

A Thanksgiving to Almighty God for the Fruits of the Earth and All the Other Blessings of His Merciful Providence

MOST gracious God, by whose knowledge the depths are broken up, and the clouds drop down the dew; We yield thee unfeigned thanks and praise for the return of seed-time and harvest, for the increase of the ground and the gathering in of the fruits thereof, and for all the other blessings of thy merciful providence bestowed upon this nation and people. And, we beseech thee, give us a just sense of these great mercies; such as may appear in our lives by an humble, holy, and obedient walking before thee all our days; through Jesus Christ our Lord, to whom, with thee and the Holy Ghost, be all glory and honour, world without end. AMEN.

(*The Book of Common Prayer*)

A *Prayer*

LORD, for the erring thought
Not into evil wrought;
Lord, for the wicked will,
Betrayed and baffled still;
For the heart from itself kept,
Our thanksgiving accept!
For ignorant hopes that were
Broken at our blind prayer;
For pain, death, sorrow sent,
Unto our chastisement;
For all loss of seeming good,
Quicken our gratitude!

WILLIAM DEAN HOWELLS (1837–1920)

A *Thanksgiving*

WE give thanks unto thee, O Lord, for thou art gracious and thy mercy endureth forever; thou art loving unto every man; thy tender mercy is over all thy world; thou satisfieth our mouths with good things; thy Word is a light unto our paths; thou hast sent thy Son to save us; thou dost give thy Spirit to teach us; thou liftest up them that are down. At thy right hand there are pleasures forevermore. Help us to show forth thy praise, not only with our lips, but in our lives; through Jesus Christ, our Lord. AMEN.

(*Prayers Old and New;* compiled by EDMUND S. ROUSMANIERE)

Thanksgiving

I THANK Thee that I learn
Not toil to spurn;
With all beneath the sun
It makes me one;—
For tears, whereby I gain
Kinship with human pain;
For Love, my comrade by the dusty ways,
I give Thee Praise.

EMILY READ JONES

A Home Prayer for Thanksgiving

FOR health and home and happy days,
The gifts of laughter and of wit,
We thank Thee, O God.

For companioning memories . . .
Like a walled-in garden to our troubled minds,
We thank Thee, O God.

For Love's enduring patience
And for Friendship's years the same,
We thank Thee, O God.

For our given sense of Beauty . . .
To plunder with our eyes as forage the pirate bees,
We thank Thee, O God.

For the sure knowledge
That some things are True beyond gain or loss,
We thank Thee, O God.

For suffering which has forged our souls by hammer and by heat
To understand the strength of the Cross,
We thank Thee, O God.

For One Man,
We thank Thee, O God.

For the kind Hand in which Thou holdest us, spared and free,
Forgiven in failure, sustained by the touch of Thy Mercy and Thy Hope,
We thank Thee, O God.

D. B. A.

O GOD of Love, we yield thee thanks for whatsoever thou hast given us richly to enjoy: for health and vigor, for the love and care of home, for joys of friendship, and for every good gift of happiness and strength. We praise thee for all thy servants who by their example and encouragement have helped us on our way, and for every vision of thyself which thou hast ever given us in sacrament or prayer; and we humbly beseech thee that all these thy benefits we may use to thy service and to the glory of thy holy Name; through Jesus Christ, thy Son, our Lord. AMEN.

(*Prayers Old and New*; compiled by EDMUND S. ROUSMANIERE)

V. AT THE CROSSROADS

Dedication

V. AT THE CROSSROADS

DEDICATION

GOD warms his hands at man's heart when he prays.

Masefield, *Widow in the Bye Street,* Part IV

IN some particular place, if it be only in one's mind, one's allegiance or loyalty finds a time to present its cause. For some the church is the place. For others a setting is found in the confidence of a friend. For another it may be in the quiet resolve of a calm and composed will. Each of us apparently has his particular place where he sees his obligations and commits himself to play his part. Usually some sense of "oughtness" compels us. "Here I stand," said Martin Luther. "They shall not pass," a once-united nation pledged. "What shall I say, Father, save me from this hour? But for this cause came I unto this hour."

Every day is a day of commitments. We do not deliver ultimatums to fortune or fate to cheer ourselves with a front of bravado. We assume a supporting strength in choosing the right as we see it. If we are later defeated and go down, there still remains something we have won—the inner conviction that we did not side-step or compromise. We feel the right choice will yet be vindicated—"Still standeth God within the shadow, keeping watch above his own." The right choice may be the lonely choice, but it never leaves one altogether alone.

D. B. A.

Dedication

TEACH us, good Lord, to serve Thee as Thou deservest; to give and not to count the cost; to fight and not to heed the wounds; to toil and not to seek for rest; to labour and not to ask for any reward, save that of knowing that we do Thy will; through Jesus Christ our Lord. AMEN.

ST. IGNATIUS LOYOLA (1491–1556)

Through rigorous self-discipline and constant contemplation, through following the example of Christ and the saints, St. Ignatius Loyola willed to become a saint and became one. His vivid companionship with God was interrupted only when he attended to the affairs of men. His Order of Jesuits, his Constitutions, his Spiritual Exercises, before publication were submitted to the severest divine scrutiny.

O GOD of peace, we turn aside from an unquiet world, seeking rest for our spirits and light for our thoughts. We bring our work to be sanctified, our wounds to be healed, our sins to be forgiven, our hopes to be renewed, our better selves to be quickened. O Thou, in whom there is harmony, draw us to thyself, and silence the discords of our wasteful lives. Thou who art one in all, and in whom all are one, take us out of the loneliness of self, and fill us with the fulness of Thy truth and love. Thou whose greatness is beyond our highest praise, lift us above our common littleness and our daily imperfections; send us visions of the love that is in Thee and of the good that may be in us. AMEN.

(*Source unverified*)

The Tree of Life

God be in my head
  And in my understanding;

God be in my eyes
  And in my looking;

God be in my mouth
  And in my speaking;

God be in my heart
  And in my thinking;

God be at my end
  And at my departing.

PINTO AND WRIGHT, No. 198, *The Sarum Primer* (1538)

TAKE, O Lord, and receive my entire liberty, my memory, my understanding, and my whole will. All that I am, all that I have, Thou hast given me, and I will give it back again to Thee to be disposed of according to Thy good pleasure. Give me only Thy love and Thy grace; with Thee I am rich enough, nor do I ask for aught besides. AMEN.

ST. IGNATIUS LOYOLA (1491–1556)

. . . WHAT else can I, a lame old man, do but sing hymns to God? If I were a nightingale I would act the part of a nightingale; if a swan, the part of a swan; but since I am a reasonable creature, it is my duty to praise God. This is my business. I do it. . . .

Lift up your head, at last, as free from slavery. Dare to look up to God and say, "Make use of me for the future as Thou wilt. I am of the same mind: I am equal with Thee. I refuse nothing that seems good to Thee. Lead me whither Thou wilt. Clothe me in whatever dress Thou wilt. . . .

If death overtakes me . . . it is enough for me if I can stretch out my hands and say, "The opportunities which Thou hast given me of comprehending and following the rules of Thy administration I have not neglected. As far as in me lay I have not dishonored Thee. . . . I thank Thee that Thou hast brought me into being. I am satisfied with the time that I have enjoyed the things which Thou hast given me. Receive them back again, and assign them to whatever place Thou wilt; for they were all Thine and Thou gavest them to me.

EPICTETUS (*ca.* 60–120)

Born in Phrygia, Epictetus lived for some time as a slave in the household of a favorite of Nero. Having somehow gained his freedom, he became a famous teacher of Stoic philosophy.

O Master, Let Me Walk with Thee

O MASTER, let me walk with Thee
In lowly paths of service free;
Tell me Thy secret; help me bear
The strain of toil, the fret of care.

Help me the slow of heart to move
By some clear winning word of love;
Teach me the wayward feet to stay,
And guide them in the homeward way.

Teach me Thy patience; still with Thee
In closer, dearer company,

In work that keeps faith sweet and strong,
In trust that triumphs over wrong.

In hope that sends a shining ray
Far down the future's broadening way,
In peace that only Thou canst give,
With Thee, O Master, let me live.

WASHINGTON GLADDEN (1836–1918)

O ETERNAL GOD, sanctify my body and soul, my thoughts and my intentions, my words and actions, that whatsoever I shall think, or speak, or do, may be by me designed for the glorification of Thy Name, and by Thy blessing, it may be effective and successful in the work of God, according as it can be capable.

Lord, turn my necessities into virtue; the works of nature into the works of grace; by making them orderly, regular, temperate; and let no pride or self-seeking, no covetousness or revenge, no little ends and low imaginations, pollute my spirit, and unhallow any of my words and actions; but let my body be a servant of my spirit, and both body and spirit servants of Jesus; that, doing all things for Thy glory here, I may be partaker of Thy glory hereafter, through Jesus Christ our Lord. AMEN.

JEREMY TAYLOR (1613–1667)

Jeremy Taylor was the author of Holy Living *and* Holy Dying, *books full of reasonable counsel and devotional encouragement and written in exquisitely quaint English. His* Liberty of Prophesying *is of primary importance for the religious and political thought of his day. As rector and bishop he suffered for his loyalty to the royal cause.*

❁

Mon seul Sauveur, que vous pourrais-je dire?
Vous connaissez tout ce que je désire;
Rien n'est caché devant votre savoir;
Le plus profond du coeur vous pouvez voir:
Par quoi à vous seulement je soupire.

MARGUERITE DE NAVARRE (1492–1549)

Marguerite de Navarre, sister of François I, diplomat and eminent author, was described by Marot in these words: "Corps féminin, coeur d'homme, et tête d'ange."

Conclusion of an Address to the Deity Asclepios

WE rejoice in thy divine salvation because thou hast shown thyself wholly to us: we rejoice that thou hast deigned to consecrate us to eternity, while we are still in these mortal bodies. We have known thee, oh true life of the life of man. . . . Adoring thy goodness, we make this our only prayer . . . that thou wouldst be willing to keep us all our lives in the love of thy knowledge.

ATTRIBUTED TO APULEIUS (b. *ca.* 125)

O MERCIFUL Lord, who hast made of one Blood and redeemed by one Ransome all Nations of Men, let me never harden my heart against any that partake of the same Nature and Redemption with me, but grant me an Universal Charity towards all Men. Give me, O Thou Father of Compassions, such a tenderness and meltingness of Heart that I may be deeply affected with all the Miseries and Calamities outward or inward of my Brethren, and diligently keep them in Love: Grant that I may not only seek my own things, but also the things of others. O that this mind may be in us all, which was in the Lord Jesus, that we may love as Brethren, be Pitiful and Courteous, and endeavour heartily and vigorously to keep the

Unity of the Spirit in the Bond of Peace, and the God of Grace, Mercy and Peace be with us all. AMEN.

THOMAS À KEMPIS (1380–1471)

O GOD, our everlasting hope, as disciples of One Who had not where to lay His head, may we freely welcome the toils and sufferings of our humanity, and seek only strength to glorify the cross Thou layest on us. Every work of our hand may we do unto Thee; in every trouble trace some lights of Thine; and let no blessing fall on dry and thankless hearts. Redeeming the time, may we fill every waking hour with faithful duty and well-ordered affections, as the sacrifice which Thou hast provided. Fill us with patient tenderness for others, seeing that we also are in the same case before Thee; and make us ready to help, and quick to forgive. And then, fix every grace, compose every fear, by a steady trust in Thine eternal realities. Grant this, O Heavenly Father, for the sake of Jesus Christ, our Lord and Saviour. AMEN.

JAMES MARTINEAU (1805–1900)

James Martineau was a philosopher and historian of philosophy, a theologian and historian of theology, a thoughtful preacher, possibly the leading Unitarian of his day, a man of wide and varied friendships and of spacious ideas, numbering among his companions such scientists as Thomas Huxley and such statesmen as John Morley.

My Prayer

GREAT God, I ask thee for no meaner pelf
Than that I may not disappoint myself;
That in my action I may soar as high
As I can now discern with this clear eye.

And next in value, which thy kindness lends,
That I may greatly disappoint my friends,
Howe'er they think or hope that it may be,
They may not dream how thou'st distinguished me.

That my weak hand may equal my firm faith,
And my life practise more than my tongue saith;
That my low conduct may not show,
Nor my relenting lines,
That I thy purpose did not know,
Or overrated thy designs.

HENRY DAVID THOREAU (1817–1862)

For Love of God

O LORD, grant us to love Thee; grant that we may love those that love Thee; grant that we may do the deeds that win Thy love. Make the love of Thee to be dearer to us than ourselves, than our families, than wealth, and even than cool water. AMEN.

MOHAMMED (570?–632)

A prayer related by Mohammed as heard on the lips of David in Paradise. Quoted by Dean Stanley.

The words of Rábi'a's prayer: All-knowing Lord,
Make this world's goods the portion of thy foes
And Paradise thy followers' reward;
But as for me, remote from these and those
I stand, for ever free.
Losing both worlds, I count the loss as light
If but one instant I may be thy friend;

Content I take from thee such beggar's plight—
From thee my true content, wealth without end,
Thyself thy gift to me.

Translation by Sir Frederick Pollock from the Persian poetical version of the prayer of Rábi'a, female mystic of Islam.

WE beseech Thee, our most gracious God, preserve us from the cares of this life, lest we should be too much entangled therein; also from the many necessities of the body, lest we should be ensnared by pleasure; and from whatsoever is an obstacle to the soul, lest, being broken with troubles, we should be overthrown. Give us strength to resist, patience to endure, and constancy to persevere; for the sake of Jesus Christ our Lord and Saviour. AMEN.

THOMAS À KEMPIS (1380–1471)

Before Action

BY all the glories of the day,
And the cool evening's benison,
By the last sunset touch that lay
Upon the hills when the day was done,
By beauty lavishly outpoured,
And blessing carelessly received,
By all the days that I have lived,
Make a soldier, Lord.

By all of all men's hopes and fears,
And all the wonders poets sing,
The laughter of unclouded years,
And every sad and lovely thing,
By the romantic ages stored
With high endeavor that was his,

By all his mad catastrophes,
Make me a man, O Lord.

I, that on my familiar hill,
Saw with uncomprehending eyes
A hundred of thy sunsets spill
Their fresh and sanguine sacrifice,
Ere the sun swings his noon-day sword
Must say goodbye to all of this—
By all delights that I shall miss,
Help me to die, O Lord!

WILLIAM NOEL HODGSON

O LORD, let me not henceforth desire health or life, except to spend them for Thee, with Thee, and in Thee. Thou alone knowest what is good for me; do, therefore, what seemeth Thee best. Give to me, or take from me; conform my will to Thine; and grant that, with humble and perfect submission, and in holy confidence, I may receive the orders of Thine eternal Providence; and may equally adore all that comes to me from Thee; through Jesus Christ our Lord. AMEN.

BLAISE PASCAL (1623–1662)

Blaise Pascal was a mathematician and a deeply and mystically religious member of the Port Royal Group. In his Thoughts *he nurtures the personal devotional life. In his* Provincial Letters *he chastises lower forms of Jesuitism.*

O HEAVENLY Father, the Father of all wisdom, understanding, and true strength, I beseech Thee, for Thy only Son our Savior Christ's sake, look mercifully upon me, wretched creature, and send Thine Holy Spirit into my breast; that not only I may understand according to Thy wisdom, how this temptation is to be borne off, and with what answer it is to be beaten back; but also, when I must join to fight in the field for the glory of Thy name, that then I, being strengthened with the defence of Thy right hand, may manfully stand in the confession of Thy faith, and of Thy truth, and may continue in the same unto the end of my life, through the same our Lord Jesus Christ. AMEN.

BISHOP RIDLEY (1500–1555)

One of the earliest and most consistent of the reformers, Nicholas Ridley was Master of Pembroke College (Cambridge), King's chaplain, Canon of Canterbury, a preacher of power. On Queen Mary's accession he was sent to Oxford with Latimer and Cranmer and burned at the stake, encouraged by Latimer's words: "Be of good comfort, Master Ridley, and play the man. We shall this day light such a candle by God's grace in England as shall never be put out." The above prayer was composed by Bishop Ridley during the imprisonment that preceded his burning at the stake.

DEAR Lord and Father of mankind,
Forgive our foolish ways!
Reclothe us in our rightful mind,
In purer lives thy service find,
In deeper reverence, praise.

In simple trust like theirs who heard,
Beside the Syrian sea,
The gracious calling of the Lord,
Let us, like them, without a word,
Rise up and follow thee.

O Sabbath rest by Galilee!
O calm of hills above,
Where Jesus knelt to share with thee
The silence of eternity
Interpreted by love!

Drop thy still dews of quietness,
Till all our strivings cease:
Take from our souls the strain and stress,
And let our ordered lives confess
The beauty of thy peace.

Breathe through the heats of our desire
Thy coolness and thy balm;
Let sense be dumb, let flesh retire;
Speak through the earthquake, wind, and fire,
O still, small voice of calm.

John Greenleaf Whittier
(1807–1892)

GRANT, I pray, O Lord, that with that lowliness of mind which befits my humble condition, and that elevation of soul which Thy majesty demands, I may ever adore Thee; may I continually live in that fear which Thy justice inspires, in that hope which Thy clemency permits. May I submit myself to Thee as All-powerful, leave myself in Thy hands as All-wise, and turn unto Thee as All-perfect and good. I beseech Thee, most merciful Father, that Thy most vivid fire may purify me, that Thy clearest light may illuminate me, and that purest love of Thine may so advance me that, held back by no mortal influence, I may return safe and happy to Thee.

Vittoria Colonna (1490–1547)

A member of a noble Roman family, standing high among the leaders of the Revival of Learning in Italy, Vittoria Colonna was a friend and intellectual companion of Michelangelo and other scholars and statesmen of her day.

JESUS, Son of God . . . Christ, son of man, by the divine blood that thou didst shed for us we swear to spend our own to the last drop when we are men . . . that children may not be forsaken any more . . . that no more mothers may be wronged and go hungry and be ashamed to carry their children in their arms.

A prayer from The Kingdom of God, *a Drama in Three Acts by G. Martinez Sierra, played in America during the season of 1928–29. The leading character, Sister Gracia, was played by Miss Ethel Barrymore.*

The scene is the closing one of the play, showing the interior of an orphanage in Spain. Sister Gracia is the head of the institution. There has been a shortage of food, and at last, when there are not even peppers for the watery broth, the older boys start a mutiny, declaring that they will find food outside if they have to pillage the shops. Gradually Sister Gracia quells the riot and leads the children in the words of this prayer, which ends the play.

BLESSED Lord, Who for our sakes wast content to bear sorrow and want and death, grant unto us such a measure of Thy Spirit that we may follow Thee in all self-denial and tenderness of soul. Help us by Thy great love to succour the afflicted, to relieve the needy and destitute, to comfort the feeble-minded, to share the burdens of the heavy-laden, and ever to see Thee in all that are poor and desolate; through Jesus Christ our Lord. AMEN.

BISHOP WESTCOTT (1825)

A Prayer

Let me do my work each day, and if the
Darkened hours of despair overcome me,
May I not forget the strength that comforted
Me in the desolation of other times. May I

Still remember the bright hours that found me
Walking over the silent hills of my childhood,
Or dreaming on the margin of the quiet river,
When a light glowed within me
And I promised my early God to have
Courage amid the tempests of the changing years.
Spare me from the bitterness and sharp passion
Of unguarded moments. May I not forget
That poverty and riches are of the spirit.
Though the world knows me not,
May my thoughts and actions be such
As shall keep me friendly with myself.
Lift up my eyes from the earth and let me
Not forget the uses of the stars.
Forbid that I should judge others lest
I condemn myself.
Let me not feel the glamour of the world,
But walk calmly in my path. Give me
A few friends who will love me for what I am,
And keep ever burning before my vagrant steps
The kindly light of hope; and though
Age and infirmity overtake me, and I
Come not within sight of the castle of my dreams,
Teach me still to be thankful for life,
And for Time's olden moments that are
Good and sweet; and may the evening twilight
Find me gentle still.

MAX EHRMANN (1903)

O LORD, let us not live to be useless; for Christ's sake. AMEN.

JOHN WESLEY (1703–1791)

COME, O Lord, in much mercy down into my soul, and take possession and dwell there. A homely mansion, I confess, for so glorious a Majesty, but such as Thou art fitting up for the reception of Thee, by holy and fervent desires of Thine own inspiring. Enter then, and adorn, and make it such as Thou canst inhabit, since it is the work of Thy hands. Give me Thine own self, without which, though Thou shouldst give me all that ever Thou hast made, yet could not my desires be satisfied. Let my soul ever seek Thee, and let me persist in seeking, till I have found, and am in full possession of Thee. AMEN.

ST. AUGUSTINE (354–430)

An incessant searcher for truth through the philosophies and religions of his day, equally ardent in the study of Scripture, into St. Augustine's life flowed the learning and experience of the past; out of his life poured influences which determined most of medieval and much of modern political and religious thought.

NOW is my soul troubled; and what shall I say? Father, save me from this hour: but for this cause came I unto this hour.

Father, glorify thy name.

John XII:27–28

Litany

GIVE me Thy grace;
Not for the shouting assault when my banner advances;
Not for the thunder of hooves and the tempest of lances.
Keep Thou my face
Calm in the heart-breaking crash of the overturned dream.
When to my mouth comes the sickening, salt taste of fear,
And over the tumult and cries of the vanquished I hear
The hurrying wings of the Furies their hideous scream—
Give me Thy steadfastness then, oh God. Give me Thy grace!

Give me Thy mirth;
Not for the sun and the sky and the summer wind's laughter,
Not for the meeting of friends and the wine that flows after,
But when the earth
Hardens to iron and the winds of adversity blow,
When the past walks, a terrible ghost, and the future is vain,
Give me Thy bright gift of laughter to flaunt before pain;
Give me Thy smile to fling stark in the teeth of the foe;
Give me the flame of Thy manhood,
God. Give me Thy mirth.

Hear me, oh Lord!
Teach me to stand on my feet in the final black hour;
Turn Thou my eyes unafraid to the oncoming power.
Give me a sword!
Grant that I cry for no shield to withstand his bleak blade,
But a hilt in my hand and an edge that the foeman may feel;
Let me pass to the chime and the chant and the clangor of
steel,
That you see and rejoice in the soul of the man you have made;
This is my prayer to You, God of Men.
Hear me, oh Lord!

F. F. Van de Water

Prayer of Sir Thomas More

ILLUMINE, good Lord, my heart! Glorious God! Give me from henceforth Thy Grace, so to set and fix firmly mine heart upon Thee, that I may say with St. Paul, the world is crucified to me, and I unto the world. Take from me all vainglorious minds, and all appetites of mine own praise. Give me, good

Lord, a humble, lowly, quiet, peaceable, patient, charitable, kind, tender and pitiful mind; and in all my works and words and thoughts, to have a taste of Thy Holy Spirit. Give me a full faith, a firm hope, a fervent charity, and a love to Thee incomparably above the love to myself. May I love nothing to Thy displeasure, but everything in order to Thee! Give me a longing to be with Thee; not for avoiding the calamities of this wicked world, nor so much the pains of purgatory, nor of hell; nor so much for the attaining of the choice of heaven, in respect of mine own commodity, as even for a very love to Thee!

SIR THOMAS MORE (1478–1535),
His Latin Diary

Executed on Tower Hill because he would not sign the document declaring Henry VIII Supreme Head of the Church in England, Sir Thomas More was, with Erasmus and Colet, one of the three Oxford Reformers. A layman of wide learning; a devoted son, father, and husband; a lawyer, member of Parliament, and Chancellor; a man of spotless daily life; a thoughtful and faithful Romanist.

For Unity with the Divine Purpose

ETERNAL God, Who committest to us the swift and solemn trust of life; since we know not what a day may bring forth, but only that the hour for serving Thee is always present, may we wake to the instant claims of Thy holy will, not waiting for to-morrow, but yielding to-day. Consecrate with Thy presence the way our feet may go, and the humblest work will shine, and the roughest place be made plain. Lift us above unrighteous anger and mistrust, into faith, and hope, and charity, by a simple and steadfast reliance on Thy sure will. In all things draw us to the mind of Christ, that Thy lost image may be traced again, and Thou mayest own us as at one with Him and Thee, to the glory of Thy great Name. AMEN.

JAMES MARTINEAU (1805–1900)

DEAREST Jesus! Teach me to be generous, teach me to love Thee as Thou deservest, to give and not to count the cost, to fight and not to heed the wounds, to toil and not to seek for rest, to labor and not to ask for reward, save to feel that I do Thy will, my God. AMEN.

(*God and I*)

Prayer of St. Thomas Aquinas before Study

GRANT me grace, O merciful God, to desire ardently all that is pleasing to Thee, to examine it prudently, to acknowledge it truthfully, and to accomplish it perfectly, for the praise and glory of Thy name. AMEN.

ST. THOMAS AQUINAS (1225–1274)

A Dominican of gigantic body, admired and befriended by Louis IX, of vast and accurate learning, of deep personal piety, St. Thomas Aquinas was certain that reason would corroborate the truths of revelation.

LORD we pray Thee that Thou wilt open our eyes to behold the heaven that lies about us, wherein they walk who, being born to the new life, serve Thee with the clearer vision and the greater joy; through Jesus Christ our Saviour. AMEN.

BISHOP CHARLES L. SLATTERY
(1867–1930)

A *Prayer*

KEEP me from bitterness. It is so easy
To nurse sharp bitter thoughts each dull dark hour!

Against self-pity, Man of sorrows, defend me,
With Thy deep sweetness and Thy gentle power.
And out of all this hurt of pain and heartbreak
Help me to harvest a new sympathy
For suffering human kind, a wiser pity
For those who lift a heavier cross with Thee.

(*Source unverified*)

Martha

YEA, Lord!—Yet some must serve!
Not all with tranquil heart
Even at thy dear feet,
Wrapped in devotion sweet,
May sit apart!

Yea, Lord!—Yet some must bear
The burden of the day,
Its labor and its heat,
While others at thy feet
May muse and pray!

Yea, Lord!—Yet some must do
Life's daily task-work; some
Who fain would sing, must toil
Amid earth's dust and moil,
While lips are dumb!

Yea, Lord!—Yet man must earn,
And woman bake the bread;
And some must watch and wake
Early for others' sake,
Who pray instead!

Yea, Lord!—Yet even Thou
  Hast need of earthly care.
I bring the bread and wine
To Thee, a guest divine—
  Be this my prayer!

JULIA C. DORR (1825–1913)

For the Vision of His Beauty

BLESS us, O God, we pray thee, with the vision of thy being and beauty; that in the light of it we may learn to think thine own thoughts after thee, and in the strength of it may do our work without haste and without rest; through Jesus Christ our Lord. AMEN.

(*Prayers Old and New;* compiled by EDMUND S. ROUSMANIERE)

O LORD God and Father, Thou knowest how blind we are to Thy presence, how dead to Thy purpose and deaf to Thy call, grant us to feel Thy guiding hand through all the scattered details of our daily life, in all the tumult to hear Thy still small voice, and in all dimness of our spirits to have a sense of Thine everlasting arms upbearing us, so that, being willing to spend and be spent in Thy service, we may accomplish all that Thou wouldest have us do, and at the last find fulfilment in the perfect freedom of Thy sole sovereignty, through Jesus Christ Thy Son our Lord. AMEN.

(*A Chain of Prayers across the Ages*)

The Higher Good

FATHER, I will not ask for wealth or fame,
Though once they would have joyed my carnal sense;

I shudder not to bear a hated name,
Wanting all wealth, myself my sole defence,
But give me, Lord, eyes to behold the truth,
A seeing sense that knows the eternal right;
A heart with pity filled and gentlest ruth;
A manly faith that makes all darkness light;
Give me the power to labor for mankind;
Make me the mouth of such as cannot speak;
Eyes let me be to groping men, and blind;
A conscience to the base; and to the weak
Let me be hands and feet; and to the foolish, mind;
And lead still further on such as thy kingdom seek.

THEODORE PARKER (1810–1860)

Son of a Lexington farmer, educated at Harvard, unprepossessing in appearance, as child and man convinced that God spoke directly to him and that inner evidence was superior to any other, in social and religious conviction Theodore Parker was in advance of Unitarians of his day, finding in Jesus the true example of worship and conduct—both possible to men.

Litany

O LORD, open thou our minds to see ourselves as thou seest us, or even as others see us and we see others, and from all unwillingness to know our infirmities,

Save us and help us

We humbly beseech thee, O Lord.

From weariness in continuing struggles, from despondency in failure and disappointment, from over-burdened sense of unworthiness, from morbid fancies of imaginary back-slidings, raise us to a lively hope and trust in thy presence and mercy, in the power of faith and prayer; and from all exaggerated fears and vexations,

Save us and help us
We humbly beseech thee, O Lord.

From pride and self-will, from desire ever to have our own way in all things, from overweening love of our own ideas and blindness to the value of others; from resentment against opposition and contempt for the claim of others; enlarge the generosity of our hearts and enlighten the fairness of our judgments; and from all selfish arbitrariness of temper,

Save us and help us
We humbly beseech thee, O Lord.

Give us knowledge of ourselves, our powers and weaknesses, our spirit, our sympathy, our imagination, our knowledge, our truth; teach us by the standard of thy Word, by the judgments of others, by examinations of ourselves; give us earnest desire to strengthen ourselves continually by study, by diligence, by prayer and meditation; and from all fancies, delusions, and prejudices of habit, or temper, or society,

Save us and help us
We humbly beseech thee, O Lord.

Finally, O Lord, we humbly beseech thee, blot out our past transgressions, heal the evils of our past negligences and ignorances, make us amend our past mistakes and misunderstandings; uplift our hearts to new love, new energy and devotion, that we may be unburthened from the grief and shame of past faithlessness to go forth in thy strength to persevere through success and failure, through good report and evil report, even to the end; and in all the time of our tribulation, in all the time of our prosperity,

Save us and help us
We humbly beseech thee, O Lord.

The Southwell Litany, Bishop George Ridding

Prayer from "Rabbi Ben Ezra"

BUT I need, now as then,
Thee, God, who mouldest men!
And since, not even while the whirl was worst,
Did I,—to the wheel of life
With shapes and colors rife,
Bound dizzily,—mistake my end, to slake Thy thirst;

So, take and use thy work,
Amend what flaws may lurk,
What strain o' the stuff, what warpings past the aim!
My times be in Thy hand!
Perfect the cup as planned!
Let age approve of youth, and death complete the same!

ROBERT BROWNING (1812–1889)

VI. FOR EVERYDAY LIFE

VI. FOR EVERYDAY LIFE

A. PRAYERS TO BE USED IN ANY FAMILY

"IS IT that the soul living here as in her prison-house strives after something boundless like herself, and finding it nowhere still renews the search?"

THOMAS CARLYLE to his mother

IN THE MORNING

O LORD, our heavenly Father, Almighty and everlasting God, who hast safely brought us to the beginning of this day; defend us in the same with thy mighty power; and grant that this day we fall into no sin, neither run into any kind of danger; but that all our doings, being ordered by thy governance, may be righteous in thy sight; through Jesus Christ our Lord. AMEN.

(*The Book of Common Prayer*)

Just for Today

LORD, for tomorrow and its needs,
I do not pray;
Keep me, my God, from stain of sin
Just for today.

Let me both diligently work,
And duly pray.
Let me be kind in word and deed,
Just for today.

Let me be slow to do my will,
Prompt to obey;
Help me to sacrifice myself
Just for today.

And if today my tide of life
Should ebb away,
Give me Thy Sacraments divine,
Sweet Lord, today.

So for tomorrow and its needs
I do not pray,
But keep me, guide me, love me, Lord,
Just for today.

(*The Anglo-Catholic Prayer Book*)

A Home Prayer

O LORD, grant that each one who has to do with me today may be the happier for it.

Let it be given me each hour today what I shall say, and grant me the wisdom of a loving heart that I may say the right thing rightly.

Help me to enter into the mind of everyone who talks with me, and keep me alive to the feelings of each one present. Give me a quick eye for little kindnesses that I may be ready in doing them and gracious in receiving them. Give me a quick perception of the feelings and needs of others, and make me eager-hearted in helping them. AMEN.

(*Prayers, New and Old*)

A Twelfth Century Prayer

THANKS be to thee, my Lord Jesus Christ,
For all the benefits thou hast given me,
For all the pains and insults thou hast borne for me.
O most merciful Redeemer, Friend, and Brother,
May I know thee more clearly,
May I love thee more dearly,
May I follow thee more nearly. AMEN.

(*Prayers, New and Old*)

Two Prayers by Dr. Arnold, Headmaster of Rugby

O LORD, I have a busy world around me; eye, ear and thought will be needed for all my work to be done in that busy world. Now, ere I enter upon it, I commit eye, ear and thought to Thee! Do Thou bless them and keep their work Thine, such as through Thy natural laws my heart beats and my blood flows without any thought of mine for them, so my spiritual life may hold on its course at those times when my mind cannot consciously turn to Thee to commit each particular thought to Thy service. Hear my prayer for my dear Redeemer's sake. AMEN.

Composed for his own daily use at the School.

O LORD, Who by Thy holy Apostle hast taught us to do all things in the name of the Lord Jesus and to Thy glory, give Thy blessing, we pray Thee, to this our daily work that we may do it in faith and heartily, as to the Lord and not unto men. All our powers of body and mind are Thine, and we would fain devote them to Thy service. Sanctify them and the work in which they are engaged; let us not be slothful but fervent in spirit, and do Thou, O Lord, so bless our efforts that they may bring forth in us the fruits of true wisdom. Strengthen the faculties of our minds and dispose us to exert them, but let us always remember to exert them for Thy glory, and for the furtherance of Thy kingdom, and save us from all pride and vanity and reliance upon our own power and wisdom. Teach us to seek after truth and enable us to gain it; but grant that we may ever speak the truth in love—that, while we know earthly things, we may know Thee and be known by Thee, through and in Thy Son Jesus Christ. Give us this day Thy Holy Spirit, that we may be Thine in body and spirit in all our work and all our refreshments, through Jesus Christ, Thy Son, our Lord. AMEN.

DR. THOMAS ARNOLD (1795–1842)
Read every morning by Dr. Arnold in the Sixth Form.

Morning Prayer

ALMIGHTY God, our Father and Preserver! We give Thee thanks that of Thy goodness Thou hast watched over us the past night and brought us to this day. We beseech Thee strengthen and guard us by Thy Spirit that we may spend it wholly in Thy service, aiming at Thy glory and the salvation of our fellow men. And even as Thou sheddest now the beams of the sun upon the earth to give light unto our bodies, so illuminate our souls with the brightness of Thy Spirit to guide us in the paths of Thine obedience. May all our purpose be this day to honor and serve Thee; may we look for all prosperity to Thy blessing only, and seek no object but such as may be pleasing in Thy sight. Enable us, O Lord, while in labor for the body and the life that now is, ever to look beyond unto that heavenly life which Thou hast promised Thy children. Defend us in soul and body from all harm. Guard us against the assaults of the devil and deliver us from any danger that may beset us. And seeing it is a small thing to have begun well except we also persevere, take us, O Lord, unto Thy good keeping this day and all our days. Continue and increase Thy grace within us, until we shall be perfectly united with the glory of Thy Son, Jesus Christ, our Lord, the Sun of Righteousness, who shall replenish our souls with his eternal light and gladness. And that we may obtain all these mercies be pleased to cast out of Thy remembrance all our past offences, and of Thy boundless mercy forgive them, as Thou hast promised those who call upon Thee in sincerity and truth. Hear us, O God, our Father, and Redeemer, through Jesus Christ our Lord. In whose name we pray, as he has taught us, "Our Father Who art in heaven," etc. AMEN.

JOHN CALVIN (1509–1564)

The Huguenot leader Admiral Coligny was in the act of repeating this prayer with his chaplain when assassins broke into his room and murdered him on the morning of St. Bartholomew's Day, 1572. At the time, Coligny was confined to his bed with wounds received in an attack on his life just two days before.

At Morning

MY God, I offer Thee
All Thou appointest me;
All that the day may bring
Of joy or suffering;
All that Thou givest to-day;
All that Thou takest away;
All Thou would'st have me be;
My God, I offer Thee.

At Noon

Lord, in Thy pierced hands
I lay my heart;
Lord, at Thy pierced feet

I choose my part;
Lord, in Thy wounded side
Let me abide.

At Night

Now that the day doth end,
My spirit I commend
To Thee, my Lord, my Friend.
Into Thy hands, yea, Thine,
Those glorious hands benign,
Those human hands divine,
My spirit I resign.

Anonymous

IN THE EVENING

SAVIOUR, again to Thy dear Name we raise
With one accord our parting hymn of praise;
We stand to bless Thee ere our worship cease,
Then, lowly kneeling, wait Thy word of peace.

Grant us Thy peace through this approaching night,
Turn Thou for us its darkness into light;
From harm and danger keep Thy children free,
For dark and light are both alike to Thee.

Grant us Thy peace upon our homeward way;
With Thee began, with Thee shall end the day;
Guard Thou the lips from sin, the hearts from shame,
That in this house have called upon Thy Name.

Grant us Thy peace throughout our earthly life,
Our balm in sorrow, and our stay in strife;
Then, when Thy voice shall bid our conflict cease,
Call us, O Lord, to Thine eternal peace.

J. Ellerton (1866)

O GOD, Who hast drawn over weary day the restful veil of night, enfold us in Thy heavenly peace. Lift from our hands our tasks, and all through the night carry in Thy care the full weight of our burdens and sorrows: that in untroubled slumber we may press our weariness close to Thy strength, and win new power for the morrow's duties from Thee, Who givest to Thy beloved in sleep, through Jesus Christ our Lord. AMEN.

(*Acts of Devotion*)

Evening Prayer

O MERCIFUL God! Eternal Light shining in darkness. Thou Who dispellest the night of sin and all blindness of heart, since Thou hast appointed the night for rest and the day for labor, we beseech Thee grant that our bodies may rest in peace and quietness, that afterward they may be able to endure the labor they must bear. Temper our sleep that it be not disorderly, that we may remain spotless both in body and soul, yea that even our sleep itself may be to Thy glory. Enlighten the eyes of our understanding that we may not sleep in death but always look for deliverance from this misery. Defend us against all assaults of the devil and take us into Thy holy protection. And although we have not passed this day without greatly sinning against Thee, we beseech Thee to hide our sins with Thy mercy as Thou hidest all things on earth with the darkness of the night, that we may not be cast out from Thy presence. Relieve and comfort all those who are afflicted in mind, body, or estate. Through Jesus Christ, our Lord. AMEN.

JOHN CALVIN (1509–1564)

John Knox, the Scottish reformer and religious leader, died repeating this prayer.

SAVIOUR, breathe an evening blessing,
Ere repose our spirits seal;
Sin and want we come confessing;
Thou canst save, and thou canst heal.
Though the night be dark and dreary,
Darkness cannot hide from thee;
Thou art he who, never weary,
Watchest where thy people be.

Though destruction walk around us,
Though the arrows past us fly,
Angel-guards from thee surround us;
We are safe, if thou art nigh.
Be thou nigh, should death o'ertake us;
Jesus, then our refuge be,
And in Paradise awake us,
There to rest in peace with thee.

JAMES EDMESTON (1820)

These lines were written by a professional surveyor and architect. His hobby was to write religious poetry. He is credited with having composed two thousand hymns. While reading a description of a party of explorers in Abyssinia, he was struck by the account of their singing an evening hymn when the day's march was ended. He determined to write a hymn of his own which should be a prayer for forgiveness and protection at the end of the day, and composed the above stanzas.

THE shadows of the evening hours
Fall from the darkening sky;
Upon the fragrance of the flowers
The dews of evening lie.

Before Thy throne, O Lord of heaven,
We kneel at close of day;

Look on Thy children from on high,
And hear us while we pray.

The sorrows of Thy servants, Lord,
Oh, do not Thou despise,
But let the incense of our prayers
Before Thy mercy rise.

The brightness of the coming night
Upon the darkness rolls;
With hopes of future glory chase
The shadows on our souls.

Slowly the rays of daylight fade:
So fade within our heart
The hopes in earthly love and joy,
That one by one depart.

Slowly the bright stars, one by one,
Within the heavens shine:
Give us, O Lord, fresh hopes in heaven,
And trust in things divine.

Let peace, O Lord, Thy peace, O God,
Upon our souls descend;
From midnight fears, and perils, Thou
Our trembling hearts defend:

Give us a respite from our toil;
Calm and subdue our woes;
Through the long day we labor, Lord,
Oh, give us now repose.

ADELAIDE ANNE PROCTER (1825–1864)

In her day Adelaide Procter was the most popular poet in England next to Alfred Tennyson. The daughter of "Barry Cornwall"

(Bryan Waller Procter), the friend of Dickens, she inspired the "golden-tressed Adelaide" of her father's poem. Her most popular poem was "The Lost Chord." In 1851 she and her two sisters followed John Henry Newman into the Church of Rome.

ABIDE with me: fast falls the eventide;
The darkness deepens; Lord, with me abide:
When other helpers fail, and comforts flee,
Help of the helpless, oh, abide with me.

Swift to its close ebbs out life's little day;
Earth's joys grow dim, its glories pass away,
Change and decay in all around I see;
O Thou Who changest not, abide with me.

I need Thy presence every passing hour;
What but Thy grace can foil the tempter's power?
Who, like Thyself, my guide and stay can be?
Through cloud and sunshine, Lord, abide with me.

I fear no foe, with Thee at hand to bless:
Ills have no weight, and tears no bitterness.
Where is death's sting? Where, grave, thy victory?
I triumph still, if Thou abide with me.

Hold Thou Thy cross before my closing eyes:
Shine through the gloom, and point me to the skies:
Heaven's morning breaks, and earth's vain shadows flee:
In life, in death, O Lord, abide with me.

HENRY FRANCIS LYTE (1847)

The author of this popular hymn was a clergyman burdened by frail health. Forced to go to the Mediterranean every winter to avoid the rigors of the English climate, in the year 1847 he preached his farewell sermon. Immediately on returning to his study after service he sat down and wrote "Abide with Me." Leaving the manuscript with a member of his family, the following day he left Devonshire for Italy. Shortly after his arrival he was stricken with a fatal illness and died in Nice.

The music associated with "Abide with Me" was composed by William Henry Monk. It is his best-known melody. He wrote it in ten minutes, to be included with the manuscript of Hymns Ancient and Modern *which lay on his desk waiting to be sent to the publisher.*

GRACIOUS Father, be pleased to touch our hearts in time with trouble, with sorrow, with sickness, with disappointment, with anything that may hinder them from being hard to the end, and leading us to eternal ruin. AMEN.

DR. THOMAS ARNOLD (1795–1842)
From a prayer used on Sunday evening in the School-House.

Evening Prayer

I LIFT my heart to Thee, O God, Thou Fountain of Eternal Life, and give Thee thanks through Jesus Christ Thy beloved Son, for having protected and preserved me this day from all mischief that might have befallen me. I commend to Thy disposal my condition and employment, together with the work of my hands, and humbly repose them on Thee. Let my mind only delight in Thee in Thy temple, and let Thy good angel stay with me that I may rest safely in Thy power, and under Thy protection. AMEN.

I, a poor unworthy creature, come before Thee, O great and holy God, and lift up mine eyes to Thee. . . . And though it is but a strange child which was disobedient unto Thee, yet now it desireth to be obedient; and doth now infold itself with its desire unto that Word which became man, which became flesh and blood, and hath opened a gate for my soul to the clear face of Thy strength and power.

And he shall find all that he can ask, and that as deep as the mind of man is able to reach.

JAKOB BOEHME (1575–1624)

GOD, be patient with me, and make those who love me patient. Forgive, and help them to forgive, my weak resolve, my stubborn pride. Father, I know how I hurt Thee, and them, when I am unreasonable and demanding, when I lose my temper over trivial things. Make me stronger, O God; help me to keep the promises I make at night to Thee and to them to mend my ways on the morrow. Help me to be patient and forgiving with them as Thou art and they are with me. When I am in the wrong give me the grace to admit it wholly, neither offering excuses nor trying to shift the blame. Make me more honest in my thinking, more charitable in my opinions. Father, in Thy mercy Thou hast given me the love of family and friends; in Thy mercy help me to be worthy of it, for Thy dear Son's sake. AMEN.

Anonymous

An Evening Collect

LIGHTEN our darkness, we beseech thee, O Lord; and by thy great mercy defend us from all perils and dangers of this night; for the love of thy only Son, our Saviour, Jesus Christ. AMEN.

(*The Book of Common Prayer*)

GOD, that madest earth and heaven,
  Darkness and light;
Who the day for toil hast given,
  For rest the night:
May Thine angel-guards defend us,
Slumber sweet Thy mercy send us,
Holy dreams and hopes attend us,
  This livelong night.

Guard us waking, guard us sleeping,
  And, when we die,
May we in Thy mighty keeping,
  All peaceful lie:
When the last dread call shall wake us,
Do not Thou, our God, forsake us,
But to reign in glory take us
  With Thee on high.

R. HEBER, 1827, AND R. WHATELEY, 1855

O LORD, support us all the day long of this troublous life until the shadows lengthen and the evening comes, and the busy world is hushed, and the fever of life is over, and our work is done. Then in Thy mercy grant us a safe lodging and a holy rest, and peace at the last. AMEN.

JOHN HENRY, CARDINAL NEWMAN (1801–1890)

WATCH Thou, dear Lord, with those who wake, or watch, or weep to-night, and give Thine angels charge over those who sleep. Tend Thy sick ones, O Lord Christ. Rest Thy weary ones. Bless Thy dying ones. Soothe Thy suffering ones. Pity Thine afflicted ones. Shield Thy joyous ones. And all, for Thy Love's sake. AMEN.

ST. AUGUSTINE (354–430)

A Lullaby Prayer

Ik ga slapen, ik ben moe,
Sluit mijn oojes beide toe,
Heere, houd ook deze nacht,
Over mij getrouw de wacht.

Booze daad ik heb gedaan,
Ziehet Heere, toch niet aan,
Schoon mijn zonden vele zijn,
Maak om Jezus wil mij rein.

Weary now, I go to sleep,
Eyes both closed for slumber deep,
Lord wilt Thou, my constant friend,
Me, Thy child, this night defend.

Evil deeds that I have done,
Lord, do Thou not look upon,
Many though my sins may be,
Clean, for Jesus' sake, make me.

Used for many generations in the Netherlands and by Dutch people in America.

The Day Is Dying in the West

DAY is dying in the west;
Heaven is touching earth with rest;
Wait and worship while the night
Sets the evening lamps alight,
Through all the sky.

Refrain

Holy, holy, holy, Lord God of Hosts!
Heaven and earth are full of Thee;
Heaven and earth are praising Thee,
O Lord most high!

Lord of life, beneath the dome
Of the universe, Thy home,
Gather us, who seek Thy face
To the fold of Thy embrace,
For Thou art nigh.

While the deepening shadows fall,
Heart of love, enfolding all,
Through the glory and the grace
Of the stars that veil Thy face,
Our hearts ascend.

When forever from our sight
Pass the stars, the day, the night,
Lord of Angels, on our eyes,
Let eternal morning rise,
And shadows end.

MARY A. LATHBURY (1877)

An Evening Commendation

INTO Thy hands, O Lord, I commend my spirit, this night and forevermore. AMEN.

(*Anglo-Catholic Prayer Book*)

FAMILY AND HOME PRAYERS

LORD, behold our family here assembled. We thank Thee for this place in which we dwell; for the love that unites us; for the peace accorded us this day; for the hope with which we expect the morrow; for the health, the work, the food and the bright skies that make our lives delightful; for our friends in all parts of the earth, and our friendly helpers in this foreign isle.

Let peace abound in our small company. Purge out of every heart the lurking grudge. Give us grace and strength to forbear and persevere. Offenders, give us the grace to accept and to forgive offenders. Forgetful ourselves, help us to bear cheerfully the forgetfulness of others.

Give us courage, gaiety and the quiet mind. Spare to us our friends, soften to us our enemies. Bless us, if it may be, in all our innocent endeavours. If it may not, give us the strength to encounter that which is to come, that we be brave in peril, constant in tribulation, temperate in wrath, and in all changes of fortune and down to the gates of death, loyal and loving one to another.

As the clay to the potter, as the windmill to the wind, as children of their sire, we beseech of Thee this help and mercy for Christ's sake. AMEN.

ROBERT LOUIS STEVENSON (1850–1894)

This prayer was written while Stevenson, gravely ill with tuberculosis, was a voluntary exile in Samoa.

O ETERNAL God, help us faithfully to fulfill our duties to thee and to each other. Put far from us all unkind thoughts, anger, and evil speaking. Give us tender hearts, full of affection and sympathy toward all. Preserve us from selfishness, and grant that day by day, walking in love, we may grow up into the likeness of thy blessed Son, Jesus Christ our Lord. AMEN.

(*Prayers, New and Old*)

GIVE me a good digestion, Lord,
And also something to digest.
Give me a healthy body, Lord,
With sense to keep it at its best.

Give me a healthy mind, Lord,
To keep the good and pure in sight,
Which, seeing sin, is not appalled,
But finds a way to set it right.

Give me a mind that is not bored,
That does not whimper, whine or sigh;
Don't let me worry overmuch
About the fussy thing called I.

Give me a sense of humor, Lord,
Give me the grace to see a joke,
To get some happiness from life
And pass it on to other folk.

Anonymous. From a tablet in Chester Cathedral, England

Prayers for Grace in Little Things

LORD of all pots and pans and things; since I've no time to be
A saint by doing lovely things or watching late with Thee,
Or dreaming in the dawnlight or storming heaven's gates,
Make me a saint by getting meals, and washing up the plates.

Altho I must have Martha's hands, I have a Mary mind;
And when I black the boots and shoes, Thy sandals, Lord, I find.
I think of how they trod the earth, what time I scrub the floor;
Accept this meditation, Lord, I haven't time for more.

Warm all the kitchen with Thy love, and light it with Thy
peace;
Forgive me all my worrying, and make all grumbling cease.
Thou Who didst love to give men food, in room or by the sea,
Accept this service that I do—I do it unto Thee.

Anonymous

A Family Grace

IN the breaking of bread, O God, we give Thee thanks, and in friendship keep Thee in remembrance, through Jesus Christ our Lord. AMEN.

EDMUND S. ROUSMANIERE

A Family Grace

BLESS, O Lord, this food to our use, and us to Thy service, and make us ever mindful of the needs of others. For Christ's sake. AMEN.

(*Prayers, New and Old*)

A Wedding in the Home

ALL-WISE, All-Great, whose ancient plan
Ordained the woman for the man,
Look down, O Lord! on these who now
Before Thy sacred altar bow.

Almighty Ruler, in whose hand
The morrow and its issues stand,
Whate'er the lot Thy will assign
We can but kneel; our all is Thine.

Summer and winter, seed and grain,
The joy unhoped that comes of pain,
The unknown ill, that good we call—
Thou in Thy balance metest all.

Throughout their lifelong journey still,
Guide Thou these two in good and ill,
And where-so-'er the way extend,
Be with them, Father, to the end.

AUSTIN DOBSON (1840–1921)

A Wedding in the Home

O GOD, bless Thy servants who are about to be joined together this day in holy matrimony; keep them, we beseech Thee, under the protection of Thy good providence, and make them to have a perpetual fear and love of Thy holy name. Look, O Lord, mercifully upon them from heaven, and bless them; that they obeying Thy will and always being in safety under Thy protection, may abide in Thy love unto their lives' end; through Jesus Christ our Lord. AMEN.

(*Family Prayer Book of the Church of Ireland*, 1895)

FOR A BIRTHDAY

A Birthday Thought

I ASK and wish not to appear
  More beauteous, rich or gay:
Lord, make me wiser every year,
  And better every day.

CHARLES LAMB (1775–1834)

WE beseech Thee, Lord, open Thy heavens; from thence may Thy gifts descend to him. Put forth Thine own hand from heaven and touch his head. May he feel the touch of Thy Hand, and receive the joy of the Holy Spirit, that he may remain blessed for evermore. AMEN.

ST. ETHELWOLD (963)

FOR PARENTS

AS we give thanks for the infinite value of children, so let us pray for Fathers and Mothers and for all of us through whom Children receive their first thoughts of God.

That we may have the love of parents and the wisdom of teachers, that our lives may be ruled by simplicity, gladness and sympathy, and that we may guide by the constraining influence of love rather than by the restraint of fear.

That by the Inspiration of Thy Loving Spirit we may direct the thoughts of our children through curiosity to wonder, through fairies to angels, through the imagination of the delights of playtime to the worship of the joys of the Eternal. . . .

May the grace of courage, gaiety, and the quiet mind, with all such blessedness as belongeth to the children of the Father in Heaven, be ours to the praise of the Father, Son and Holy Spirit, Who ever liveth and reigneth One God. World without end. AMEN.

(From "*Litany on the Grace of Childhood*," *in Acts of Devotion*)

Mother Prayer

"LORD, make my loving a guard to them,
  Day and night
Let never pathway be hard to them,
  Keep all bright!
Let not a stone or a thorn for them

Wound their ease,
All of the pain I have borne for them
Spare to these!"
So I would pray for them,
Kneeling to God
Night and day for them.

"Lord, let the griefs life must bring to them
Make them strong.
Keep their hearts white though pain cling to them
Their life long.
Let all the joys Thou dost keep from them
At Thy will
Give them the power to reap from them
Courage still!"
So must I ask for them,
Leaving to God
His good task for them.

MARGARET WIDDEMER

CHILDREN'S PRAYERS

Child's Morning Hymn

FATHER, we thank Thee for the night,
And for the pleasant morning light;
For rest and food and loving care
And all that makes the world so fair.

Help us to do the things we should,
To be to others kind and good;
In all we do in work and play,
To love Thee better day by day.

REBECCA J. WESTON

A Boy's or Girl's Prayer

O GOD, give me clean hands, clean words, and clean thoughts. Help me to stand for the hard right against the easy wrong. Save me from habits that harm. Teach me to work as hard and play as fair in thy sight alone, as if all the world saw. Forgive me when I am unkind, and help me to forgive those who are unkind to me. Keep me ready to help others at some cost to myself; send me chances to do some good every day, and so grow more like Christ. AMEN.

(*Prayers, New and Old*)

Prayer to Our Guardian Angel

O ANGEL of God, my guardian dear,
To whom His love commits me here,
Ever this day be at my side,
To light and guard, to rule and guide. AMEN.

Anonymous

A Child's Prayer for Kindness to Animals

O LORD Jesus Christ, who hast taught us that without our Father in heaven no sparrow falls to the ground, help us to be very kind to all animals and our pets. May we remember that Thou wilt one day ask us if we have been good to them. Bless us as we take care of them. For Thy sake. AMEN.

(*A Chain of Prayer across the Ages*)

The Bells of Heaven

'TWOULD ring the bells of Heaven
The wildest peal for years,
If Parson lost his senses

And people came to theirs,
And he and they together
Knelt down with angry prayers
For tamed and shabby tigers,
And dancing dogs and bears,
And wretched, blind pit-ponies,
And little hunted hares.

RALPH HODGSON

Little Jesus

LITTLE Jesus, wast Thou shy
Once, and just so small as I?
And what did it feel like to be
Out of Heaven, and just like me?
Didst Thou sometimes think of *there*,
And ask where all the angels were?
I should think that I would cry
For my house all made of sky;
I would look about the air,
And wonder where my angels were;
And at waking 'twould distress me—
Not an angel there to dress me!
Hadst Thou ever any toys,
Like us little girls and boys?
And didst Thou play in Heaven with all
The angels that were not too tall,
With stars for marbles? Did the things
Play *Can you see me?* through their wings?
And did Thy Mother let Thee spoil
Thy robes, with playing on *our* soil?
How nice to have them always new
In Heaven, because 'twas quite clean blue!

Didst Thou kneel at night to pray,
And didst Thou join Thy hands, this way?
And did they tire sometimes, being young,
And make the prayer seem very long?
And dost Thou like it best, that we
Should join our hands to pray to Thee?
I used to think, before I knew,
The prayer not said unless we do.
And did Thy Mother at the night
Kiss Thee, and fold the clothes in right?
And didst Thou feel quite good in bed,
Kissed, and sweet, and Thy prayers said?

Thou canst not have forgotten all
That it feels like to be small:
And Thou know'st I cannot pray
To Thee in my father's way—
When Thou wast so little, say,
Couldst Thou talk Thy Father's way?—
So, a little Child, come down
And hear a child's tongue like Thy own;
Take me by the hand and walk,
And listen to my baby-talk.
To Thy Father show my prayer
(He will look, Thou art so fair),
And say: "O Father, I, Thy Son,
Bring the prayer of a little one."

And He will smile, that children's tongue
Has not changed since Thou wast young.

FRANCIS THOMPSON (1859–1907)

A Child's Grace

HERE a little child I stand
Heaving up my either hand;
Cold as paddocks though they be,
Here I lift them up to Thee,
For a benison to fall
On our meat and on us all. AMEN.

ROBERT HERRICK (1591–1674)

A Child's Grace

GOD is great and God is good,
And we thank Him for our food.
By His hand we all are fed.
Give us, Lord, our daily bread.
AMEN.

For Evening

NOW the day is over,
Night is drawing nigh;
Shadows of the evening
Steal across the sky;

Jesus, give the weary
Calm and sweet repose;
With thy tenderest blessing
May our eyelids close.

Grant to little children
Visions bright of thee;
Guard the sailors tossing
On the deep, blue sea.

Comfort every sufferer
  Watching late in pain;
Those who plan some evil
  From their sins restrain.

Through the long night watches,
  May thine angels spread
Their white wings above me,
  Watching round my bed.

When the morning wakens,
  Then may I arise
Pure, and fresh, and sinless
  In thy holy eyes. AMEN.

SABINE BARING-GOULD (1834–1924)

This evening hymn was written for the children of the Sunday school of a church in Yorkshire and was first published in 1861 in Hymns Ancient and Modern. *This is the edition that gave to the world "Abide with Me," set to music by* William H. *Monk.*

A Child's Evening Prayer

NOW I lay me down to sleep,
I pray the Lord my soul to keep;
If I should die before I wake,
I pray the Lord my soul to take.

This famous and popular prayer for children is of great antiquity. It has been traced back to a manuscript of the twelfth century, no doubt in an original Latin form.

The prayer came to the American Colonies from England and was printed in the New England Primer. *The older version ran its first line "Now I lay me down to take my sleep." It appears that way in a reprint of 1777. In the 1784 edition, however, we find the present version, "Now I lay me down to sleep." In the 1814 printing of the* Primer *another wording was given to the second line, "I pray Thee, Lord, my soul to keep"; but that change did not find favor, and ever since then the little quotation has remained unchanged from one generation of children to another.*

A *Child's Evening Prayer*

LORD, keep us safe this night,
  Secure from all our fears;
May Angels guard us while we sleep
  Till morning light appears.

(*Prayers, New and Old*)

A *Child's Evening Prayer*

JESUS, tender Shepherd, hear me;
  Bless Thy little lamb to-night;
Through the darkness be Thou near me;
  Keep me safe till morning light.

All this day Thy hand has led me,
  And I thank Thee for Thy care;
Thou hast warmed me, clothed and fed me;
  Listen to my evening prayer!

Let my sins be all forgiven;
  Bless the friends I love so well:
Take us all at last to heaven,
  Happy there with Thee to dwell.

MARY DUNCAN (1839)

B. PRAYERS FOR SPECIAL NEEDS

FOR ENLIGHTENMENT

O LORD, keep us sensitive to the grace that is around us. May the familiar not become neglected. May we see Thy goodness in our daily bread, and may the comforts of our home take our thoughts to the mercy-seat of God; through Jesus Christ. AMEN.

J. H. JOWETT (1864–1923)

WE must praise Thy goodness, that Thou hast left nothing undone to draw us to Thyself. But one thing we ask of Thee, our God, not to cease Thy work in our improvement. Let us tend towards Thee, no matter by what means, and be fruitful in good works, for the sake of Jesus Christ our Lord. AMEN.

LUDWIG VAN BEETHOVEN (1770–1827)

LORD, in this hour of tumult,
Lord, in this night of fears,
Keep open, oh keep open
My eyes, my ears!

Not blindly, not in hatred,
Lord, let me do my part;
Keep open, oh, keep open,
My mind, my heart!

HERMANN HAGEDORN

FOR RIGHT LIVING

O LORD, renew our spirits and draw our hearts unto Thyself, that our work may not be to us a burden, but a delight; and give us such a mighty love to Thee as may sweeten all our obedience. Oh, let us not serve Thee with the spirit of bondage as slaves, but with cheerfulness and gladness of children, delighting ourselves in Thee, and rejoicing in Thy work for the sake of Jesus Christ. AMEN.

BENJAMIN JENKS

WHO can tell what a day may bring forth? Cause us, therefore, gracious God, to live every day as if it were to be our last, for that we know not but it may be such. Cause us to live so at present as we shall wish we had done when we come to die. O grant that we may not die with any guilt upon our consciences, or any known sin unrepented of, but that we may be found in Christ, Who is our only Saviour and Redeemer. AMEN.

THOMAS À KEMPIS (1380–1471)

FOR PROTECTION

ALMIGHTY and everlasting God, be Thou present with us in all our duties, and grant the protection of Thy presence to all that dwell in this house, that Thou mayest be known to be the Defender of this household and the Inhabitant of this dwelling; through Jesus Christ our Lord. AMEN.

(*Gelasian Sacramentary*, 494)

ALMIGHTY God, Who seest that we have no power of ourselves to help ourselves; keep us both outwardly in our bodies, and inwardly in our souls; that we may be defended from all adversities which may happen to the body, and from all evil thoughts which may assault and hurt the soul; through Jesus Christ our Lord. AMEN.

(*Gregorian Sacramentary*, 590)

JESU, lover of my soul,
  Let me to Thy bosom fly,
While the nearer waters roll,
  While the tempest still is high:
Hide me, O my Saviour, hide,
  Till the storm of life be past;
Safe into the haven guide,
  Oh, receive my soul at last!

Other refuge have I none,
  Hangs my helpless soul on Thee;
Leave, ah! leave me not alone,
  Still support and comfort me:
All my trust on Thee is stayed;
  All my help from Thee I bring;
Cover my defenseless head
  With the shadow of Thy wing.

Plenteous grace with Thee is found,
  Grace to cleanse from every sin;
Let the healing streams abound,
  Make and keep me pure within:
Thou of life the fountain art,
  Freely let me take of Thee:
Spring Thou up within my heart,
  Rise to all eternity.

CHARLES WESLEY (1708–1788)

The story connected with this hymn is that Charles and his brother John Wesley, together with a friend, held an open-air meeting on the common. This aroused the anger of the townsfolk. They attacked the three men with stones so that they were forced to run for their lives. At nightfall, finding shelter in a springhouse, there Charles Wesley composed this hymn. His is credited with six thousand other hymns and rivals Watts as the greatest hymn writer of the English language.

Like his brother John, the founder of Methodism, Charles Wesley was an Anglican by birth and an Anglican throughout his ministry, but, unlike John, Charles preferred the normal Anglican methods of religious expression and found in them no limit to religious freedom.

For a Person, or Persons, Going to Sea

O ETERNAL God, who alone spreadest out the heavens, and rulest the raging of the sea; We commend to thy almighty protection, thy servant, for whose preservation on the great deep our prayers are desired. Guard him, we beseech thee, from the dangers of the sea, from sickness, from the violence of enemies, and from every evil to which he may be exposed. Conduct him in safety to the haven where he would be, with a grateful sense of thy mercies; through Jesus Christ our Lord. AMEN.

(*The Book of Common Prayer*)

FOR STRENGTH AND COURAGE

O MOST merciful Lord, we beseech Thee that Thou wilt give courage to Thy soldiers, wisdom to the perplexed, endurance to sufferers, fresh vigour and interest in life to those who have lost heart, a sense of Thy Presence to the lonely, and to bless and prosper all of this household; for the sake of Christ Jesus. AMEN.

A. McCheane (*nineteenth century*)

O GOD, whose spirit is to be known by those whose hearts are thankful, and who makest cheerfulness to be a companion of strength . . . lift up our hearts, we beseech Thee, to a joyous confidence in Thy care. Teach us to know that a shadow is only a shadow, because the light of eternal goodness shines behind the object of our fears. Where there is love in life, teach us to find it; help us to trust it; give it to us to grow in the power of it. So may our lives present a cheerful ray to our fellowmen. We ask it in the name of him whose life was the light of men, the same Jesus Christ. AMEN.

D. B. A.

The Prayer

O LORD of Courage grave,
O Master of this night of Spring!
Make firm in me a heart too brave
To ask Thee anything.

JOHN GALSWORTHY (1867–1933)

By One Suffering from Rheumatism

DEAR Lord of Courage and Fortitude, if I must have rheumatism, so help me by Thy divine grace to bear it in such a manner that I do not make every other person in the house feel the pain. Give me the grace to refuse to describe over and over again the misery and pangs that belong to me alone. Strengthen in me the desire to get well, that I may not even be tempted to live in the pity and sympathy that is expected to be extended to an invalid. May I remember continually that pains in nerves are multiplied by pains in description. AMEN.

ALLEN A. STOCKDAL

GRANT us grace to rest from all sinful deeds and thoughts, to surrender ourselves wholly unto Thee, and to keep our souls still before Thee like a still lake; that so the beams of Thy grace may be mirrored therein, and may kindle in our hearts the glow of faith, and love, and prayer. May we, through such stillness and hope, find strength and gladness in Thee, O God, now and for evermore. AMEN.

JOACHIM EMBDEN (1595)

FOR INNER PEACE

O GOD, from whom all holy desires, all good counsels, and all just works do proceed; Give unto thy servants that peace which the world cannot give; that our hearts may be set to obey thy commandments, and also that by thee, we, being defended from the fear of our enemies, may pass our time in rest and quietness; through the merits of Jesus Christ our Saviour. AMEN.

(*The Book of Common Prayer*)

For the Secret of Peace

HEAVENLY Father, in Whom is no darkness at all, nor any shadow that is cast by turning, forgive our feverish ways—our anxieties, our fears, our uncertainties. We are like children walking wilfully and blindly in darkness while the world without is ablaze with light. Open our eyes that we may see Thee; and our minds that we may understand and know Thee. Help us to make the great adventure of faith, and discover the secret of peace, in finding Thee, Thou great Companion of our souls. AMEN.

(*Prayers for Faith and Trust*, compiled by EDMUND S. ROUSMANIERE)

Inner Peace

O GOD, who art the author of peace and lover of concord, in knowledge of whom standeth our eternal life, whose service is perfect freedom; Defend us thy humble servants in all assaults of our enemies; that we, surely trusting in thy defence, may not fear the power of any adversaries, through the might of Jesus Christ our Lord. AMEN.

(*The Book of Common Prayer*)

For the Peace Which Passeth Understanding

O GOD, who art Love, grant to Thy children to bear one another's burdens in perfect good will, that Thy peace which passeth understanding may keep our hearts and minds in Christ Jesus our Lord. AMEN.

(*Source unverified*)

For Inner Peace

ALMIGHTY God, who changes not, amid the strifes of the world grant us Thy peace; in all its changefulness be Thou our stay; deliver us from its vanities, and enable us to find our chief good in Thee. Let all bitterness and wrath, and evil-speaking be put away from us; may we be kind-hearted, and learn to forgive one another, even as Thou hast forgiven us, through Jesus Christ our Lord. AMEN.

(*Source unverified*)

FOR CONFIDENCE

O THOU, who hast ordered this wondrous world, who knowest all things in earth and heaven, so fill our hearts with trust in Thee that by night and by day, at all times and in all seasons, we may without fear commit those who are dear to us to Thy never-failing love for this life and the life to come. Through Jesus Christ, our Lord. AMEN.

(*Prayers Old and New,* compiled by EDMUND S. ROUSMANIERE)

I WILL lay me down in peace and take my rest, for it is Thou, Lord, only that makest me dwell in safety.

(*Psalm* 4:8)

For Confidence

O LORD Jesus Christ, Who art the Way, the Truth, and the Life, we pray Thee suffer us not to stray from Thee, Who art the Way, nor to distrust Thee, Who art the Truth, nor to rest in any other thing than Thee, Who art the Life. Teach us by Thy Holy Spirit what to believe, what to do, and wherein to take our rest. For Thine own name's sake we ask it. AMEN.

DESIDERIUS ERASMUS (1466?–1536)

Uncertain whether he would die for the Faith, Erasmus apparently was ready to die for books, thinking that information and clear thinking would reform the Church from within. Hence his studies in the Fathers, his editions of the Greek Testament and of the Latin New Testament, his Paraphrases of the New Testament, and his handbook for daily religious living.

For Faith

O MOST loving Father, Who willest us to give thanks for all things, to dread nothing but the loss of Thee, and to cast all our care on Thee, Who carest for us, preserve us from faithless fears and worldly anxieties, and grant that no clouds of this mortal life may hide us from the light of that Love which is immortal, and which Thou hast manifested unto us in Thy Son Jesus Christ our Lord. AMEN.

WILLIAM BRIGHT (1824–1901)

IN SORROW

Prayer in Bereavement

O GOD, help me to think of Thee in this bitter trial. Thou knowest how my heart is rent with grief. In my weakness, tested so severely in soul by this visitation, I cry unto Thee, Father of all life: give me fortitude to say with Thy servant Job:

"The Lord hath given; the Lord hath taken away; blessed be the name of the Lord."

Forgive the thoughts of my rebellious soul. Pardon me in these first hours of my grief, if I question Thy wisdom and exercise myself in things too high for me. Grant me strength to rise above this trial, to bear with humility life's sorrows and disappointments. Be nigh unto me, O God. Bring consolation and peace to my soul.

Praised art Thou, O God, who comfortest the mourners. AMEN.

(*Union Prayer Book*)

HERE by the windy docks I stand alone,
But yet companioned; there the vessel goes,
And there my friend goes with it; but the wake
That melts and ebbs between that friend and me
Love's earnest is of life's all-purposeful
And all triumphant sailing, when the ships
Of wisdom loose their fretful chains and swing
Forever from the crumbled wharves of time.

(*Source unverified*)

WE seem to give him back to Thee, dear God, who gavest him to us. Yet as Thou didst not lose him in giving, so we have not lost him by his return. Not as the world giveth, givest Thou, O Lover of Souls! What Thou givest Thou takest not away. For what is Thine is ours always, if we are Thine. And life is eternal; and love is immortal, and death is only a horizon, and a horizon is nothing save the limit of our sight. Lift up, strong Son of God, that we may see further; cleanse our eyes that we may see more clearly; draw us closer to Thyself that we may know ourselves nearer to our beloved who are with Thee. And while Thou dost prepare a place for us, prepare us for that happy place, that where they are, and Thou art, we too may be. Through Jesus Christ our Lord. AMEN.

(*Author Unknown*)

O ALMIGHTY God, who hast knit together thine elect in one communion and fellowship in the mystical body of thy Son Christ our Lord; Grant us grace so to follow thy blessed Saints in all virtuous and godly living, that we may come to those unspeakable joys which thou hast prepared for those who unfeignedly love thee; through the same thy Son Jesus Christ our Lord. AMEN.

Burial Services, compiled by
JOSEPH BUCHANAN BERNARDIN

ALMIGHTY God, we entrust all who are dear to us to thy never-failing care and love, for this life and the life to come; knowing that thou art doing for them better things than we can desire or pray for; through Jesus Christ our Lord. AMEN.

Burial Services, compiled by
JOSEPH BUCHANAN BERNARDIN

O LORD, by all thy dealings with us, whether of joy or pain, of light or darkness, let us be brought to thee. Let us value no treatment of thy grace simply because it makes us happy or because it makes us sad, because it gives us or denies us what we want; but may all that thou sendest us bring us to thee; that, knowing thy perfectness, we may be sure in every disappointment thou art still loving us, in every darkness thou art still enlightening us, and in every enforced idleness thou art giving us life, as in his death thou didst give life to thy Son, our Saviour, Jesus Christ. AMEN.

Burial Services, compiled by
JOSEPH BUCHANAN BERNARDIN

A Prayer for the Sorrowing

ALMIGHTY and everlasting God, the Comfort of the sad, the Strength of sufferers, let the prayers of those that cry out of any tribulation come unto Thee, that all may rejoice to find that Thy mercy is present with them in their afflictions: through Jesus Christ our Lord. AMEN.

(*Gelasian Sacramentary*, 494)

For the Lonely

O LORD, Thou lover of souls, in whose hand is the life of every living thing, we bring before Thee in our prayers all those who are lonely in the world. Thine they are, and none can pluck them out of Thy hand. In Thy pitiful mercy let our remembrance reach them and comfort their hearts. For Thy love's sake. AMEN.

(*Prayers, New and Old*)

For Those Who Suffer

O THOU who art Love, and who seest all the suffering, injustice and misery which reign in this world; look mercifully upon the poor, the oppressed, and all who are heavy laden with labor and sorrow. Fill our hearts with deep compassion for those who suffer, and hasten the coming of thy kingdom of justice and truth. AMEN.

(*Source unverified*)

For the Homeless

O LORD, O Son of Man, who hadst not where to lay Thy head, look in Thy compassion on wandering men and women who have no home. Thou who hadst so little of the comfort of home, be with the outcast and forlorn; Thou who art the living Bread and Water, be present by the wayside at their humble meals; Thou who didst think upon the straying sheep, remember these lost ones and bring them to Thy fold. AMEN.

(*Source unverified*)

FOR STEADFASTNESS

ALMIGHTY God, who dost never change, grant that from thine unchangeableness may come our fixedness; and as year by year passes away, and the touch of change come upon us, ever in thine unchanging wisdom and love may we find a refuge. May we abide with quiet heart, knowing that we are ever within thy loving care, leaving to thee the things that are too high for us and the wisdom that is too deep for us, and looking forward fearlessly, blessing thee that thou givest us light enough for our day's work, hope enough for the night of darkness, life enough for love, until our great change comes; after which, lead thou us in the paths of eternal peace. We ask this through Jesus Christ and in his name. AMEN.

(*Prayers for Faith and Trust,* compiled by EDMUND S. ROUSMANIERE)

O LORD God, when Thou givest to Thy servants to endeavour any great matter, grant us also to know that it is not the beginning, but the continuing of the same until it be thoroughly finished, which yieldeth the true glory; through Him that for the finishing of Thy work laid down His life. AMEN.

SIR FRANCIS DRAKE (1540?–1596)

The above prayer, composed by Sir Francis Drake on the day of his famous dash into the harbor of Cádiz in 1587, was appointed to be read in all the churches of England on a Sunday in the spring of 1941.

Philip II, in the year 1587, was outfitting his Armada in the harbor of Cádiz for the projected conquest of England. Drake boldly took his own fleet into the harbor, fell upon the Spanish galleons, and set them afire. "Continuing of the same until it was thoroughly finished," despite the shore batteries, Drake sailed out again in triumph. This bold stroke delayed the sailing of the Armada a whole year. During that year Spain's great admiral, Santa Cruz, died, leaving the command of the expedition to a man totally without naval experience. That fact had much to do with the failure of the Armada in 1588 and the salvation of England.

For God's Comfort at All Times

GRANT, O Lord, that we may live in Thy fear, die in Thy favour, rest in Thy peace, rise in Thy power, reign in Thy glory; for the sake of Thy Son, Jesus Christ our Lord. AMEN.

Archbishop Laud (1573–1645)

William Laud was executed on Tower Hill for his unyielding allegiance to the government and liturgy of the Anglican Church. As Bishop and Archbishop undiplomatic, tactless, altogether blind to the contribution of nonconformity, he insisted on conformity. Of deep personal piety and supremely unselfish, "liturgical prayers were the language of his soul."

FOR HEALING

For the Sick

FOLD in Thy compassion, loving Jesus, those who are smitten with disease. Lay a healing hand upon the wounds of their souls, that inner peace may be their portion. Revive their failing strength and let life conquer death in their suffering bodies, that rejoicing in Thy mercy they may serve Thee with grateful hearts all their days upon earth. AMEN.

(*Source unverified*)

O most merciful God, who art both the Mind of Thy creation and the Father of us all, send Thy light to Thy children who grope in mental darkness and the dimness of uncertain sight. Turn the night of their distress into the morning of Thy hope, and cause them and those who watch and wait to rest confidently in Thee. We ask it in the name of Jesus Christ our Lord. AMEN.

(*Source unverified*)

O God, our Refuge in pain, our Strength in weakness, our Help in trouble, we come to Thee in our hour of need, beseeching Thee to have mercy upon this Thine afflicted servant. O loving Father, relieve his pain. Yet if he needs must suffer, strengthen him, that he may bear his sufferings with patience and as his day is, so may his strength be. Let not his heart be troubled, but shed down upon him the peace which passeth understanding. Though now for a season, if need be, he is in heaviness through his manifold trials, yet comfort him, O Lord in all his sorrows, and let his mourning be turned into joy, and his sickness into health; through Jesus Christ our only Lord and Saviour. AMEN.

(*Source unverified*)

For a Person About to Undergo an Operation

WE beseech Thee, Lord Jesus Christ, to fill the heart of thy servant with utter trust in thee, that he may have faith to say, "Though I am sometime afraid, yet put I my trust in Thee." May he feel underneath him the everlasting arms, and rest in them. By those wounds and bruises, which thou bearest for us, look graciously upon the suffering body of this thy servant, and bless the means employed for his cure, and grant that he may so patiently endure all his suffering that the wounding of his body may be to the salvation of his soul. For thy name's sake. AMEN.

(*Source unverified*)

VII. "FOR THE LOVE THAT CROWNS OUR DAYS"

Praise and Aspiration

VII. "FOR THE LOVE THAT CROWNS OUR DAYS"

PRAISE AND ASPIRATION

"THOU hast made us for Thyself, and our hearts are restless until they repose in Thee."

St. Augustine

"I HAVE felt a presence that disturbs me with a sense of elevated thoughts." From the primitive feeling of something "uncanny" to a sense of the sublime is a long reach. Yet who knowing life is not at times aware of something Other? To identify such occasional moments of perception with the Controller of the moral order may baffle our intellectual processes, but most of us have "a consciousness not merely of a moral law but of a moral law at once approved and disobeyed." Call it what you will; but from the perception of pagan feeling to the insight of the Christian mystic, a Source of Aspiration to which man *responds* has ever lifted him above himself. And, so lifted up, he has "thanked God" for it. People have been released from chains of habit and given hope for despair by this "Unknown" who will not let them go. "We never live so long in the dark that we forget what the day is like." Man has the unique power of being able to look objectively at himself. When the scientist, therefore, scrutinizes man, he must remember that he with his aesthetic, moral, and spiritual capacities is himself a specimen. So the observable data includes responsiveness to Something beyond himself. Man could not forever deceive himself into generating his own highest aspirations. It would be like playing tennis just for the exercise. The glad heart is glad not because it cries out to life and hears its own echo. It is glad because aspiration is in itself somewhat of an answer. "We love God because He first loved us."

D. B. A.

The Canticle of the Sun

O MOST high, Almighty, good Lord God, to thee belong praise, glory, honor, and all blessing!

Praised be my Lord God for all his creatures, and especially for our brother the sun, who brings us the day and who brings us the light; fair is he and shines with a very great splendor: O Lord, he signifies to us thee!

Praised be my Lord for our sister the moon, and for the stars, the which he has set clear and lovely in heaven.

Praised be my Lord for our brother the wind, and for air and cloud, calms and all weather, by the which thou upholdest life in all creatures.

Praised be my Lord for our sister water, who is very serviceable unto us and humble and precious and clean.

Praised be my Lord for our brother fire, through whom thou givest us light in the darkness; and he is bright and pleasant and very mighty and strong.

Praised be my Lord for our mother the earth, the which doth sustain us and keep us and bringeth forth divers fruits and flowers of many colors, and grass.

Praised be my Lord for all those who pardon one another for his love's sake, and who endure weakness and tribulation:

blessed are they who peaceably shall endure, for thou, O most Highest, shalt give them a crown.

Praised be my Lord for our sister the death of the body, from which no man escapeth. Woe to him who dieth in mortal sin! Blessed are they who are found walking by thy most holy will, for the second death shall have no power to do them harm.

Praise ye and bless the Lord, and give thanks unto him, and serve him with great humility.

ST. FRANCIS OF ASSISI (1182–1286)

St. Francis of Assisi, founder of the Franciscan Order, was one of the most spiritual and Christlike of the medieval saints. The son of a wealthy merchant, his earlier years were spent in the usual pastimes of the noble youth of the country. Obeying a dream, he gave away everything he possessed and lived in absolute poverty the rest of his life.

Gloria in Excelsis

GLORY be to God on high, and on earth peace, good will towards men. We praise thee, we bless thee, we worship thee, we glorify thee, we give thanks to thee for thy great glory, O Lord God, heavenly King, God the Father Almighty.

O Lord, the only-begotten Son, Jesus Christ; O Lord God, Lamb of God, Son of the Father, that takest away the sins of the world, have mercy upon us. Thou that takest away the sins of the world, receive our prayer. Thou that sittest at the right hand of God the Father, have mercy upon us.

For thou only art holy; thou only art the Lord; thou only, O Christ, with the Holy Ghost, art most high in the glory of God the Father. AMEN.

(*The Book of Common Prayer*)

For Love of God

O GOD, Who hast prepared for them that love Thee such good things as pass man's understanding; pour into our hearts such love towards Thee, that we, loving Thee above all things, may obtain Thy promises, which exceed all that we can desire; through Jesus Christ our Lord. AMEN.

(*Gelasian Sacramentary*, 494)

Salve Regina

HAIL, holy Queen, Mother of mercy, hail, our life, our sweetness, and our hope! To thee do we cry, poor banished children of Eve, to thee do we send up our sighs, mourning and weeping in this valley of tears. Turn them, most gracious advocate, thine eyes of mercy towards us; and after this our exile, show unto us the blessed fruit of thy womb, Jesus. O clement, O loving, O sweet virgin Mary.

V. Pray for us, O holy Mother of God.

R. That we may be made worthy of the Promises of Christ.

Ordered by Pope Leo XIII to be said kneeling after the celebration of Low Mass.

Magnificat

MY soul doth magnify the Lord, and my spirit hath rejoiced in God my Saviour.

For he hath regarded the lowliness of his handmaiden.

For behold, from henceforth all generations shall call me blessed.

For he that is mighty hath magnified me; and holy is his Name.

And his mercy is on them that fear him throughout all generations.

He hath showed strength with his arm; he hath scattered the proud in the imagination of their hearts.

He hath put down the mighty from their seat, and hath exalted the humble and meek.

He hath filled the hungry with good things; and the rich he hath sent empty away.

He remembering his mercy hath holpen his servant Israel; as he promised to our forefathers, Abraham and his seed for ever.

Luke I:46–55

Mary's prayer of praise and thanksgiving at the Annunciation.

Nearer, my God, to thee,
  Nearer to thee,
E'en though it be a cross
  That raiseth me;
Still all my song would be,
Nearer, my God, to thee,
  Nearer to thee.

Though like the wanderer,
  The sun gone down,
Darkness be over me,
  My rest a stone;
Yet in my dreams I'd be
Nearer, my God, to thee,
  Nearer to thee.

There let the way appear
  Steps unto heaven;
All that thou sendest me

In mercy given;
Angels to beckon me
Nearer, my God, to thee,
Nearer to thee.

Then with my waking thoughts
Bright with thy praise,
Out of my stony griefs
Bethel I'll raise;
So by my woes to be
Nearer, my God, to thee,
Nearer to thee.

Or if on joyful wing,
Cleaving the sky,
Sun, moon, and stars forgot,
Upwards I fly,
Still all my song shall be,
Nearer, my God, to thee,
Nearer to thee. AMEN.

SARAH FLOWER ADAMS (1805–1848)

The author of this familiar and prayerlike hymn was the wife of a civil engineer in London. She started her career with the dream of becoming a great actress and made an appearance as Lady Macbeth at the Richmond Theatre. But this ambition came to an end with a breakdown in health. Thereafter she devoted herself to writing religious verse. She composed this prayer not as a hymn, but as a paraphrase of Jacob's dream. Since she was a Unitarian, a circumstance that in her day was considered as ungodly as being an atheist, the evangelical churches refused for a long time to approve of "Nearer, My God, to Thee." Its great popularity and wide acceptance among all the churches came about through the work of the American composer Lowell Mason, who wrote for it the tune "Bethany." It was the favorite hymn of two Presidents of the United States, Abraham Lincoln and William McKinley; the lat-

ter died with the words on his lips. Its most heroic association is with the sinking of the Titanic *on her maiden voyage in April, 1912. As the great steamer settled deep in the water the ship's orchestra, knowing well that there was no room in the lifeboats for them, bravely kept their places. The last passengers who left the ship heard them playing "Nearer, My God, to Thee."*

For Acceptable Worship

O ALMIGHTY God, from Whom every good prayer cometh, and Who pourest out on all who desire it the spirit of grace and supplication, deliver us, when we draw nigh to Thee, from coldness of heart and wanderings of mind, that with steadfast thoughts and kindled affections we may worship Thee in spirit and in truth; through Jesus Christ our Lord. AMEN.

WILLIAM BRIGHT (1824–1901)

For Consecration

ALMIGHTY God, Who hast made all things for man, and man for Thy glory, sanctify our body and soul, our thoughts and our intentions, our words and actions, that whatsoever we shall think, or speak or do, may by us be designed to the glorification of Thy name . . . and let no pride or self-seeking, no impure motive or unworthy purpose, no little ends, and low imagination stain our spirit, and unhallow any of our words and actions. But let our body be a servant to our spirit, and both body and spirit servants of Jesus Christ. AMEN.

THOMAS À KEMPIS (1380–1471)

Te Deum Laudamus

WE praise thee, O God; we acknowledge thee to be the Lord.
All the earth doth worship thee, the Father everlasting.
To thee all Angels cry aloud; the Heavens, and all the Powers therein;
To thee Cherubim and Seraphim continually do cry,
Holy, Holy, Holy, Lord God of Sabaoth;
Heaven and earth are full of the Majesty of thy glory.
The glorious company of the Apostles praise thee.
The goodly fellowship of the Prophets praise thee.
The noble army of Martyrs praise thee.
The holy Church throughout all the world doth acknowledge thee;
The Father, of an infinite Majesty;
Thine adorable, true, and only Son;
Also the Holy Ghost, the Comforter.

THOU art the King of Glory, O Christ.
Thou art the everlasting Son of the Father.
When thou tookest upon thee to deliver man, thou didst humble thyself to be born of a Virgin.
When thou hadst overcome the sharpness of death, thou didst open the Kingdom of Heaven to all believers.
Thou sittest at the right hand of God, in the glory of the Father.
We believe that thou shalt come to be our Judge.
We therefore pray thee, help thy servants, whom thou hast redeemed with thy precious blood.
Make them to be numbered with thy Saints, in glory everlasting.

O LORD, save thy people, and bless thine heritage. Govern them, and lift them up for ever.

Day by day we magnify thee;
And we worship thy Name ever, world without end.
Vouchsafe, O Lord, to keep us this day without sin.
O Lord, have mercy upon us, have mercy upon us.
O Lord, let thy mercy be upon us, as our trust is in thee.
O Lord, in thee have I trusted; let me never be confounded.

(*The Book of Common Prayer*)

KING ZEUS, grant us the good whether we pray for it or not, but evil keep from us though we pray for it.

FORMULA QUOTED BY PLATO
(427?–347 B.C.)

DO with me as thou wilt; my will is thy will; I appeal not against thy judgments.

EPICTETUS (*ca.* 60–120)

MAY I walk, O God, in the guileless paths of life, and leave behind me a fair name for my children.

O GOD, that bringest all things to pass, grant me the spirit of reverence for noble things.

PINDAR (522–448? B.C.)

Prayer for Grace to Do the Will of God

GRANT me, most kind Jesus, Thy grace, that it may abide with me, labor with me, and persevere with me to the end.

Grant me ever to desire and to will that which is the more acceptable to thee, and pleases thee more dearly.

May thy will be mine, and my will ever follow thine, and be in closest accord with it.

May it be my one care to will and to be unwilling with thee, and may I be unable to will or not will anything but what thou willest or willest not.

Anonymous

From In Memoriam

O LIVING will that shall endure
  When all that seems shall suffer shock,
  Rise in the spiritual rock,
Flow thro' our deeds and make them pure,

That we may lift from out of dust
  A voice as unto him who hears,
  A cry above the conquer'd years
To one that with us works, and trust,

With faith that comes of self-control,
  The truths that never can be proved
  Until we close with all we loved,
And all we flow from, soul in soul.

ALFRED, LORD TENNYSON (1809–1892)

Psalm 63

(In Part)

O GOD, thou art my God; early will I seek thee: my soul thirsteth for thee, my flesh longeth for thee in a dry and thirsty land, where no water is;

To see thy power and thy glory, so as I have seen thee in the sanctuary.

Because thy lovingkindness is better than life, my lips shall praise thee.

Thus will I bless thee while I live: I will lift up my hands in thy name.

My soul shall be satisfied as with marrow and fatness; and my mouth shall praise thee with joyful lips:

When I remember thee upon my bed, and meditate on thee in the night watches.

Because thou hast been my help, therefore in the shadow of thy wings will I rejoice. . . .

LEAD me, O God, and thou my destiny,
To that one place which you will have me fill:
I follow gladly. Should I strive with Thee
A recreant, I needs must follow still.

CLEANTHES (300?–220? B.C.)

LORD, take my heart, for I cannot give it to Thee. And when Thou hast it, keep it, for I would not take it from Thee. And save me in spite of myself, for Christ's sake. AMEN.

FRANÇOIS DE LA MOTHE FÉNELON
(1651–1715)

Intellectually one of the ablest of Frenchmen, religiously François de la Mothe Fénelon was a conspicuous leader among the mystics—so much so that the Church suspected him of Quietism, the complete loss of one's self in God. He was tutor to the heir to the throne; the defender of Madame Guyon, the Quietist; and Bishop of Cambray.

Mohammedan Prayer of Adoration

Persian

SOUL of the Soul!

Neither thought nor reason comprehends Thy essence, and no one knows Thy attributes.

Souls have no idea of Thy being.

The prophets themselves sink in the dust of Thy road.

All intellect exists by Thee; has it ever yet found the path of Thy existence?

O Thou who art in the interior and in the exterior of the soul! Thou art and Thou art not what I say.

In Thy presence reason grows dizzy; it loses the thread that would direct it in Thy way.

I perceive clearly the universe in Thee, and yet discover Thee not in the world.

All beings are marked with Thy impress, but Thyself hast no impress visible;

Thou reservest the secret of Thy existence.

(*Pagan Prayers*)

Prayer for Heavenly Wisdom

O THOU, who by Mind everlasting rulest the world, Maker of lands and sky, who orderest Time to flow from the beginning, and, Thyself at rest, makest all things move; whom no external causes urge to fashion the work of fluctuating matter, but the innate Form of the Highest Good, beyond all rivalry. Thou deducest all from a heavenly pattern, Thyself most beautiful, guiding a beautiful universe by Mind, moulding it to that Image, and commanding its perfect parts to combine for the perfection of the whole. Thou bindest the elements by numbers, that Cold should match with Heat, and Dry with Moist, lest the purer flame should fly off, or the heavy things overlay all lands.

In like manner Thou bringest into being Souls, and the lesser lives, yoking things sublime to frail vehicles, which by a kindly law Thou makest to return to Thyself by virtue of their native fire.

Grant, O Father, to our minds, to climb to that august abode, grant us to visit the Fountain of the Good, grant that, finding the Light, we may open wide and fix on Thee the eyes of our souls. Scatter the mists and the heaviness of the earthly mass, and shine out with Thy own splendour: for Thou art the Serene, Thou the tranquil resting place of the pious: to behold Thee, is the aim. Thou art at once the beginning, the carrier, the guide, the pathway and the end.

BOETHIUS (*ca.* 475–524)
Translated by Padraic deBrun

Boethius was a Roman philosopher. While at the court of the King of the Ostrogoths he fell into disfavor because he defended a man who had been accused of treason. Thrown into prison, Boethius made use of the time in writing a work, De Consolatione Philosophiae, *which had a profound influence on the thought of the Middle Ages. King Alfred translated excerpts of this into Anglo Saxon.*

Prayer from the "Adieu"

FATHER of Light! to Thee I call;
My soul is dark within;
Thou who canst mark the sparrow's fall,
Avert the death of sin.
Thou, who canst guide the wandering star,
Who calm'st the elemental war,
Whose mantle is yon boundless sky,
My thoughts, my words, my crimes forgive;
And, since I soon must cease to live,
Instruct me how to die.

LORD BYRON (1788–1824)

ALMIGHTY God, Whose glory the heavens are telling, the earth His power, and the sea His might, and Whose greatness all feeling and thinking creatures everywhere herald; to Thee belongeth glory, honour, might, greatness and magnificence now and for ever, to the ages of ages, through Jesus Christ our Lord. AMEN.

(*Liturgy of St. James, second century*)

Prayer for Enlightenment

COME, Holy Ghost, fill the hearts of Thy faithful:
And enkindle in them the fire of Thy love.
Send forth Thy Spirit and they shall be created:
And Thou shalt renew the face of the earth.

O God, Who has taught the hearts of the faithful by the light of the Holy Ghost, give us by the same Spirit a love and relish of what is right and just, and the constant enjoyment of His comforts. Through Christ our Lord. AMEN.

Anonymous

WHO thou art I know not,
  But this much I know,
Thou hast set the Pleiades
  In a silver row:
Thou hast sent the trackless winds
  Loose upon their way;
Thou hast reared a colored wall
  Twixt the night and day;
Thou hast made the flowers to bloom
  And the stars to shine;
Hid rare gems of richest ore
  In the tunneled mine:
But the chief of all Thy wondrous works,

Supreme of all Thy plan,
Thou hast put an upward reach
In the heart of man.

HARRY KEMP

Hymn to Ammon Ra

Egyptian

HAIL to thee, Ammon Ra, Lord of the thrones of the earth, the oldest existence, ancient of heaven, support of all things;

Chief of the gods, Lord of truth; father of the gods, maker of men and beasts and herbs; maker of all things above and below;

Deliverer of the sufferer and oppressed, judging the poor;

Lord of wisdom, Lord of mercy; most loving, opener of every eye, source of joy, in whose goodness the gods rejoice, thou whose name is hidden.

Thou art the one, maker of all that is, the one; the only one; maker of gods and men; giving food to all.

Hail to thee, thou one with many heads; sleepless where all others sleep, adoration to thee.

Hail to thee from all creatures from every land, from the height of heaven, from the depth of the sea.

The spirits thou hast made extol thee, saying, welcome to thee, father of the fathers of the gods; we worship thy spirit which is in us.

(*Pagan Prayers*)

O JESU, Lord of Love . . . who art greater than all angels, cherubims and men, let my love unto Thee be as strong as Death, and so deep that no waters may be able to drown it.

O let it be ever endless and invincible! . . . O that no torments . . . no allurements might divide me from Thee. Let the length and breadth and height and depth of my love unto Thee be like Thine unto me. Let undrainable fountains, and unmeasurable abysses be hidden in it. Let it be more vehement than flame, more abundant than the sea, more constant than the candle in Aaron's Tabernacle that burned day and night. . . . O let it be a perpetual fire on the altar of my heart, and let my Soul itself be Thy living sacrifice.

THOMAS TRAHERNE (1637–1674)
Edited by Bertram Dobell

Thomas Traherne was in his lifetime an obscure cleric who wrote poetry only for his own pleasure. The manuscripts of his poems were unknown until about 1896, when they happened to be discovered on a bookstall. At first they were attributed to Traherne's contemporary Vaughan. Uneven in quality, they contain passages of real beauty and high spiritual fervor.

OH thou that stayst the earth and hast thy firm throne thereon, whoso'er thou art, unfathomable to human knowledge, whether thou art Zeus or the necessity of Nature, or the mind of man, to thee I raise my voice.

EURIPIDES (480–406 B.C.), *Troades*

SOCRATES: O beloved Pan and all ye other gods of this place, grant to me that I be made beautiful in my soul within, and that all external possessions be in harmony with my inner man. May I consider the wise man rich; and may I have such wealth as only the self-restrained man can endure.—Do we need anything more, Phaedrus? For me that prayer is enough.
PHAEDRUS: Let me also share in this prayer; for friends have all things in common.

PLATO (427?–347 B.C.),
Phaedrus, Conclusion

I prayed the prayer of Plato old:
God make thee beautiful within,
And let thine eyes the good behold
In everything save sin!

JOHN GREENLEAF WHITTIER (1807–1892)
My Namesake Stanza 43

Vocation

DEAR Lord,
I saw the beauty of the earth,
The trees, the flowers,
All: I saw the children's mirth,
I felt the gentle breeze.
I heard the birds' sweet call,
I loved it all:
And yet, I longed for more—
Something to fill the void
Within my soul,
Something whole;
Something—I knew not what,
Something that contained each joy:
Each, all, and yet
Where'er I turned I found alloy.
Until—Ah! sweet and wonderful
I heard Thy voice:
That I must come to Thee,
Must rest at last in Thee.
My love
I come, my heart is Thine alone,
Complete Thy Love, and take
me for Thine own.

(*Author unknown*)

An Ancient Irish Hymn

I OFFER Thee—
Every flower that ever grew,
Every bird that ever flew,
Every wind that ever blew,
Good God!
Every thunder rolling,
Every church bell tolling,
Every leaf and sod.
Laudamus Te!

I offer Thee—
Every wave that ever moved,
Every heart that ever loved,
Thee, Thy Father's Well-Beloved,
Dear Lord!
Every river dashing,
Every lightning flashing,
Like an angel's sword.
Benedicimus Te!

I offer Thee—
Every cloud that ever swept
O'er the skies, and broke and wept
In rain, and with the flow'rets slept,
My King!
Each communicant praying,
Every angel staying
Before Thy throne to sing!
Adoramus Te!

I offer Thee—
Every flake of virgin snow,
Every spring the earth below,
Every human joy and woe.
  My Love!
O Lord! And all Thy glorious
Self, o'er death victorious,
Throned in heaven above.
  Glorificamus Te!

MARY BROCAS HARRIS, *Altar of Fellowship*

Saint Patrick's Hymn before Tara

Irish

CHRIST, as a light,
Illumine and guide me!
Christ as a shield, o'ershadow and cover me!
Christ be under me! Christ be over me!
  Christ be beside me
  On left hand and right!
Christ be before me, behind me, about me!
Christ this day be within and without me!

Christ, the lowly and meek,
  Christ, the all-powerful, be
In the heart of each one to whom I speak,
  In the mouth of each who speaks to me!
    In all who draw near me,
    Or see me or hear me!

At Tara to-day, in this awful hour,
  I call on the Holy Trinity!

Glory to Him who reigneth in power,
The God of the Elements, Father, and Son,
And Paraclete Spirit, which Three are the One,
The ever-existing Divinity!

Salvation dwells with the Lord
With Christ, the Omnipotent Word.
From generation to generation
Grant us, O Lord, Thy grace and salvation!

JAMES CLARENCE MANGAN

Petition

LORD, merge my will in Yours. May it accept with love the bitter and sweet of life. Possess my intellect, that I may think of You, aspire to You, be guided by You on my journey through life.

No matter how long the years may be, let no murmur escape my lips, no unkind thoughts take shelter in my heart, no self-seeking lurk within my soul. With a smile upon my lips and a song of joy within my heart, may I walk courageously with You, my hidden Lord and Saviour, Jesus Christ. AMEN.

(*Author unknown*)

Assyrian Prayer

Assyrian

IN Heaven who is great?
Thou alone art great!
On earth who is great? Thou alone art great!
When thy voice resounds in Heaven the gods fall prostrate!
When thy voice resounds on earth, the genii kiss the dust!

(*Pagan Prayers*)

Chinese Liturgy

ONE in spirit
We invoke thee!
Hail, Amit-abha of the world!
Oh would that our merciful teacher,
Sakya-muni,
And our great father, Amit-abha,
Would now descend and be present with us.
Would that the perfect, compassionate heart would now
draw near
And receive our offerings.
May the omnipotent and omniscient Holy Spirit
Come to us while we recite these divine sentences.

(*Pagan Prayers*)

Prayer of Aeschylus
(525–456 B.C.)

ZEUS, Zeus, whate'er He be,
If this name He love to hear
This He shall be called of me,
Searching earth and sea and air.
Refuge nowhere can I find
Save him only, if my mind
Will cast off, before it die,
The burden of this vanity.

WILL DURANT, *The Life of Greece*

Ave Maria

AVE, Maria, gratia plena; Dominus tecum: benedicta tu in mulieribus, et benedictus fructus ventris tui Jesus. Sancta Maria, Mater Dei, ora pro nobis peccatoribus, nunc et in hora mortis nostrae. AMEN.

HAIL, Mary, full of grace; the Lord is with thee; blessed are thou amongst women, and blessed is the fruit of thy womb, Jesus. Holy Mary, Mother of God, pray for us sinners, now and at the hour of our death. AMEN.

The Ave Maria has been made popular through the musical compositions of Schubert, Gounod, and many other well-known composers. The English translation is also given, and in this form it is, after the Lord's Prayer, the best-loved prayer of Roman Catholics.

The Prayer of a Camper

GOD of the Hills, grant me Thy strength to go back into the cities without faltering,
Strength to do my daily task without tiring and with enthusiasm,
Strength to help my neighbor who has no hills to remember.

God of the Lake, grant me Thy peace and Thy restfulness,
Peace to bring into a world of hurry and confusion,
Restfulness to carry to the tired one whom I shall meet every day;
Content to do small things with a freedom from littleness;
Self-control for the unexpected emergency and patience for the wearisome task;
With deep depths within my soul to bear with me through the crowded places:
And the laughter of the sunny waves to brighten the cheerless spots in a long winter.

God of the Stars, may I take back the gift of friendship and of love for all.
Fill me with a great tenderness for the needy person at every turning.

Grant that in all my perplexities and every-day decisions I may keep an open mind.

God of the Wilderness, with thy pure winds from the northland, blow away my pettiness;
With the harsher winds of winter drive away my selfishness and hypocrisy;
Fill me with the breadth and the depth, and the height of Thy wilderness;
May I live out the truths which Thou hast taught me by every thought and word and deed.

(*The New Hymnal for American Youth*)

The Elixir

TEACH me, my God and King,
In all things Thee to see,
And what I do in anything
To do it as for Thee.

Not rudely, as a beast,
To run into an action;
But still to make Thee prepossessed,
And give it his perfection.

A man that looks on glasse,
On it may stay his eye:
Or if he pleaseth, through it passe,
And then the heav'n espie.

All may of Thee partake:
Nothing can be so mean
Which with his tincture, "for Thy sake,"
Will not grow bright and clean.

A servant with this clause
  Makes drudgery divine;
Who sweeps a room as for Thy laws
  Makes that and th' action fine.

This is the famous stone
  That turneth all to gold;
For that which God doth touch and owne
  Cannot for lesse be told.

GEORGE HERBERT (1593–1633)

The Gloria

GLORY be to the Father,
And to the Son,
And to the Holy Ghost;

As it was in the beginning,
Is now,
And ever shall be,
World without end.
AMEN.

Sonnet 73

LORD, make me see thy glory in every place:
  If mortal beauty sets my heart aglow,
  Shall not that earthly fire by thine burn low
Extinguisht by the great light of thy grace?

Dear Lord, I cry to thee for help, O raise
  Me from the misery of this blind woe,
  Thy spirit alone can save me: let it flow
Through will and sense, redeeming what is base.

Thou hast given me on earth this god-like soul,
And a poor prisoner of it thou hast made
Behind weak flesh-walls; from that wretched state

How can I rescue it, how my true life find?
All goodness, Lord, must fail without thy aid:
For thou alone hast power to alter fate.

MICHELANGELO (1475–1564)

The Doxology

PRAISE God, from Whom all blessings flow!
Praise Him, all creatures here below!
Praise Him above, ye heavenly host!
Praise Father, Son, and Holy Ghost! AMEN.

VIII. A HAND WITHIN OUR OWN

Guidance

VIII. A HAND WITHIN OUR OWN

GUIDANCE

PRAYER is like opening a sluice between the great ocean and our little channels, when the sea gathers itself together and flows in at full tide.

ALFRED TENNYSON

PROBABLY the greatest obstacle to doing the "will" of God is one's own will. We must first get out of our own way. A story of Lincoln during the most demanding days of the war depicts him leaving the White House for an evening walk alone. Suddenly a lad burst through a hedge and was thrown flat as he crashed into the President's long legs. Picking himself up, the lad took a pose. "Is it getting to be that a Southern gentleman can no longer walk the streets of Washington without being knocked down?" Lincoln, it is alleged, put his great hand on the lad's shoulder and said, "Son, the fellow who is in your way is inside of you."

A good deal of nonsense has been employed in identifying our own will with God's will and vice versa. "You may attribute miracles to God but not nonsense," C. S. Lewis says in his volume *The Problem of Pain.* "Nonsense remains nonsense even when we talk it about God." A "hunch" is no more God's guidance than is fortuitous circumstance. Some seem to regard God as quite too available, not altogether unlike a handy man, always about the place ready to be put to work. For the Christian, I presume God's will is definable in terms of what Jesus wanted for everyone. And the will of Jesus is seen in the Spirit he lived. With the elimination of self, or the merging of self in that will which Jesus expressed, therefore, our choices must aim to respond to that Spirit. So we shall think neither to bend God's will to our own nor to appropriate it too easily. Like the hand of a friend we earn its trusting hold on us.

D. B. A.

For Guidance

FATHER,
The path ahead is dark,
And we know not where thou wouldst have us to go.
Give us, O give us, thy gracious guidance
And a tranquil trust in thy love,
That we may walk forward through the gloom,
Unfaltering, fearless, and confident,
Having within us that divine Light
Which makest clear as day the darkest midnight,
Guiding the traveller who shall trust in thee
Safe through impenetrable forests and over trackless mountains.

(*Source unverified*)

Lead, Kindly Light

LEAD, kindly Light, amid the encircling gloom,
Lead Thou me on;
The night is dark, and I am far from home,
Lead Thou me on;
Keep Thou my feet: I do not ask to see
The distant scene; one step's enough for me.

I was not ever thus, nor prayed that Thou
Shouldest lead me on;
I loved to choose and see my path; but now
Lead Thou me on;
I loved the garish day, and, spite of fears,
Pride ruled my will. Remember not past years.

So long Thy power has blessed me, sure it still
Will lead me on
O'er moor and fen, o'er crag and torrent, till
The night is gone;
And with the morn those angel faces smile
Which I have loved long since, and lost awhile!

JOHN HENRY, CARDINAL NEWMAN
(1801–1890)

An Anglican for half his life, a Romanist for the other half, Cardinal Newman was, with Keble and Pusey and others, a leader of the Oxford Movement. As an Anglican, the author of "Lead, Kindly Light" was at first confident that Anglicanism was a pure form of Catholicism; later, suspecting it of schism, he finally accepted Romanism as the Truth and became Cardinal. Apologia pro Vita Sua, *the story of his conversion, is one of the great autobiographies.*

This, the most famous composition from Newman's pen, was written during a vacation trip in the Mediterranean. While on his way back to England in June of that year, 1833, he lay ill for three weeks with malaria in Sicily. Though still wretched in health, he managed to take passage on a fruit boat for Marseilles. This little vessel was becalmed for a whole week at sea. It was during this trying time of discomfort, illness, and waiting that Newman composed "Lead, Kindly Light."

He was sick at heart as well as in body. He felt at the time that there was much that was wrong with the Church of England and that the burden of reform would have to rest on his own shoulders. This was the "encircling gloom" of the hymn. Curiously enough, some critics found fault with this hymn because the Deity is nowhere named in its stanzas; they denounced it, therefore, as "atheistic."

O HEAVENLY Father, in Whom we live and move and have our being, we humbly pray Thee so to guide and govern us by Thy Holy Spirit, that in all the cares and occupations of our daily life we may never forget Thee, but remember that we are ever walking in Thy sight; for Thine own Name's sake. AMEN.

(*An Ancient Collect,* 440)

O GOD, by Whom the meek are guided in judgment, and light riseth up in darkness for the godly; grant us, in all our doubts and uncertainties, the grace to ask what Thou wouldst have us to do, that the spirit of wisdom may save us from all false choices, and that in Thy light we may see light, and in Thy straight path may not stumble; through Jesus Christ our Lord. AMEN.

WILLIAM BRIGHT (1824–1901)

For God's Safe Keeping

MAY the strength of God pilot us. May the power of God preserve us. May the wisdom of God instruct us. May the hand of God protect us. May the way of God direct us. May the shield of God defend us.

May the host of God guard us against the snares of the Evil One and the temptations of the world.

May Christ be with us. Christ before us. Christ in us. Christ over us. May Thy salvation, O Lord, be always ours this day and for evermore. AMEN.

ST. PATRICK (389?–461)

Saint Patrick, although the patron saint of Ireland and although his name is associated entirely with Eire, was born in Scotland, near the present town of Dumbarton. As a youth he was taken captive by the Picts and sold as a slave into Ireland. After six years he made his escape and, entering the priesthood, devoted the rest of his life to bringing all Ireland to Christianity.

King George VI closed his Christmas Day, 1939, address to the Empire thus:

I feel we may all find a message of encouragement in the lines which in my closing words I should like to read to you:

"I said to a man who stood at the gate of the year: 'Give me a light that I may tread safely into the unknown,' and he replied, 'Go out into the darkness and put your hand into the hand of God. That shall be to you better than a light and safer than a known way.'"

May that Almighty hand guide and uphold us all.

After great difficulty the above quotation was run down as occurring in the introduction to an obscure book of verses, called The Desert, *written by a Miss Minnie Haskins, a teacher of social science. The Nazi broadcaster's reaction to this passage was, "An unholy cause cannot be transformed into a holy one simply by disguising it behind a quotation from the Bible."*

LEAD us, O Father, in the paths of peace;
  Without Thy guiding hand we go astray,
And doubts appall, and sorrows still increase;
  Lead us through Christ, the true and living Way.

Lead us, O Father, in the paths of truth;
  Unhelped by Thee, in error's maze we grope,
While passion stains, and folly dims our youth,
  And age comes on, uncheered by faith and hope.

Lead us, O Father, in the paths of right;
  Blindly we stumble when we walk alone,
Involved in shadows of a darksome night,
  Only with Thee we journey safely on.

Lead us, O Father, to Thy heavenly rest,
  However rough and steep the path may be,
Through joy or sorrow, as Thou deemest best,
  Until our lives are perfected in Thee.

WILLIAM H. BURLEIGH

O ETERNAL God, who hast set within us a spirit which answers to Thine own, give us the faith to follow that image of Jesus which can keep Thy spirit so plainly before us. To our questioning hearts he is ever the answer. Teach us to be led by him in pursuit of Thee until we find, and let the whole world feel and see, that things which were cast down are being raised up, and things which had grown old are being made new, through him whose good cheer can overcome the world, the same Jesus Christ. AMEN.

D. B. A.

Prayer for Every Day

GOD, give me sympathy and sense
  And help me keep my courage high;
God, give me calm and confidence,
  And—please—a twinkle in my eye.

MARGARET BAILEY

LEAD Thou me God, Law, Reason, Motion, Life!
All names alike for Thee are vain and hollow.
Lead me—for I will follow without strife;
Or if I strive, still must I blindly follow.

CLEANTHES (300?–220? B.C.). Translated
by John Addington Symonds

These lines were inscribed on the translator's grave.

O GOD our Father, who dost exhort us to pray, and who dost grant what we ask, if only, when we ask, we live a better life; hear me, who am trembling in this darkness, and stretch forth Thy hand unto me; hold forth Thy light before me; recall me from my wanderings; and, Thou being my Guide, may I be restored to myself and to Thee, through Jesus Christ. AMEN.

ST. AUGUSTINE (354–430)

For Union with God

LORD, we know not what we ought to ask of Thee; Thou only knowest what we need; Thou lovest us better than we know how to love ourselves. O Father! give to us, Thy children, that which we ourselves know not how to ask. We would have no other desire than to accomplish Thy will. Teach us to pray. Pray Thyself in us; for Christ's sake. AMEN.

FRANÇOIS DE LA MOTHE FÉNELON
(1651–1715)

For Guidance in Speech

GRANT that no word may fall from me against my will unfit for the present need.

PERICLES (495?–429 B.C.)

Silent Devotion

O GOD, keep my tongue from evil and my lips from speaking guile. Be my support when grief silences my voice, and my comfort when woe bends my spirit. Plant humility in my soul, and strengthen my heart with perfect faith in Thee. Help me to be strong in trial and temptation and to be meek when others wrong me, that I may readily forgive them. Guide me by the light of Thy counsel, and let me ever find rest in Thee, who art my Rock and my Redeemer.

Let the words of my mouth and the meditation of my heart be acceptable in Thy sight, O Lord, my Rock and my Redeemer. AMEN.

(*Union Prayer Book*)

O BLESSED Lord, who didst walk with thy disciples through the country roads and fields of Galilee, be with thy messengers everywhere who go forth in thy name. Go before them in welcome. Be with them in fellowship upon the road. And yet as they pass onward, stay thou behind in the hearts of thy people; for thou art the same, the Beginning and the End, our Saviour and our Friend, Jesus Christ. AMEN.

(*Source unverified*)

Oraison Dominicale

XVIe *siècle*

PÈRE de nous qui es là hault ès cieux,
Sanctifié soit ton nom précieux;
Advienne tost ton sainct règne parfaict;
Ton vueil en terre ainsi qu'au ciel soit faict;
A ce iour d'hui sois nous tant debonnaire
  De nous donner notre pain ordinaire;
Pardonne nous les maulx vers toy commis,
  Comme faisons à tous nos ennemys;

Et ne, permets en ce bas territoire
　　Tentation avoir sur nous victoire;
Mais du malin cauteleux et subtil
　　Delivre nous, o père, ainsi soit-il.

Clément Marot (1495–1544)

"Oraison Dominicale" is the French title for the Lord's Prayer, frequently used in place of the Latin Pater Noster. *Clément Marot is believed to be the first to translate the Lord's Prayer into verse. He was courtier for a time during the reign of Marguerite of Navarre. His translation of the Psalms achieved great popularity among the Calvinists. Because of his sympathies with the Protestants, he was exiled for a while, but finally returned to France. His reputation is generally based on his courtly verse.*

IX. WHEN THE HEART REMEMBERS

Intercessions

IX. WHEN THE HEART REMEMBERS

INTERCESSIONS

"MORE things are wrought by prayer
Than this world dreams of. Wherefore, let thy voice
Rise like a fountain for me night and day.
For what are men better than sheep and goats
That nourish a blind life within the brain,
If, knowing God, they lift not hands of prayer
Both for themselves and those who call them friend?
For so the whole round earth is every way
Bound by gold chains about the feet of God."

TENNYSON in *Morte D'Arthur*

TO intercede, to speak on behalf of a person to God, a sort of spiritual intervention, may at the outset be best put down as a pure act of faith. "No man hath seen God at any time." If God is a Spirit, that Fatherly Power need not be seen. The Spirit is known by us in its relationship to our powers. As in friendship, the appearance of our friend does not concern us. A relationship with his spirit is what counts. Neither time nor space alters that relationship. Once grant the existence of a Divine Being, acknowledge our own spirit to be more than humanly self-created, and one is on the way to experience that Spirit which is not self. We then pray to God in His own Spirit. That a power greater than ourselves is conveyed to the person for whom we pray seems not to stand in doubt. No one can hold back the outpourings of a loving heart. Its goal in God can be no less than the love which prompted it. And in Him "in Whom we live and move and have our being," the spirit of those for whom we pray and our own spirit meet. When a friend says, "Remember me in your prayers," he is not asking for a spiritual wireless. He is acknowledging an existing spiritual relationship and fact in which he would be strengthened.

D.B.A.

The Power of Intercession

AWAY in foreign fields they wondered how
Their simple word had power—
At home the Christians two or three had met
To pray an hour.
Yes, we are always wondering, wondering how!
Because we do not see
Someone—perhaps unknown and far away—
On bended knee.

(*Prayers, New and Old*)

An Intercession

ALMIGHTY God, our Heavenly Father, Who lovest all and forgettest none, we bring to Thee our supplications for all Thy creatures and all Thy children.

For all whom we love and for whom we watch and care. For all who have blessed us with kindness and led us with patience, restored us with their sympathy and help.

We remember before Thee all on whom Thou hast laid the cross of suffering, the sick in body and the weak in mind. All who have been bereaved of relations or friends, all who are troubled by the suffering or sin of those they love; all who have met with worldly loss, that in the dark and cloudy day they may find assurance and peace in Thee.

We pray for all who are absorbed in their own grief, that they may be raised to share the sorrows of their brethren, and know the secret and blessed fellowship of the Cross.

For all who are lonely and sad in the midst of others' joys, that they may know God as their Friend and Comforter.

Remember, O Lord, the aged and infirm, all who are growing weary with the journey of life, all who are passing through the valley of shadows, that they may find that Christ the risen of the dead is with them, and that there is light at evening time.

O God our Father, hear our intercessions, answer them according to Thy will, and make us the channels of Thine infinite pity and love, for the sake of Jesus Christ Thy Son our Saviour and Redeemer. AMEN.

J. HUNTER

ALMIGHTY God, whose most dear Son went not up to joy, but first he suffered pain, and entered not unto glory before he was crucified; Mercifully grant unto thy servant, for whom our prayers are desired, that walking in the way of the Cross, he may find it none other than the way of life and peace; through Jesus Christ our Lord. AMEN.

(*Prayers*)

A Prayer for All Conditions of Men

O GOD, the Creator and Preserver of all mankind, we humbly beseech thee for all sorts and conditions of men; that thou wouldest be pleased to make thy ways known unto them, thy saving health unto all nations. More especially we pray for thy holy Church universal; that it may be so guided and governed by thy good Spirit, that all who profess and call themselves Christians may be led into the way of truth, and hold the faith in unity of spirit, in the bond of peace, and in righteousness of life. Finally, we commend to thy fatherly goodness all those who are any ways afflicted, or distressed, in mind, body, or estate; that it may please thee to comfort and relieve them, according to their several necessities; giving them patience under their sufferings, and a happy issue out of all their afflictions. And this we beg for Jesus Christ's sake. AMEN.

(*The Book of Common Prayer*)

My Prayer For You

PEACE is the test.
Grief and unrest
  Are from this world of care.
Eternal love,
From realms above,
  Is God's own gift, most fair.

Then raise your heart
Above earth's mart,
  To Him Who reigns on high.
All does He know,
Each trial and woe,
  Your every tear and sigh.

Oh, may your life
Hold naught of strife,
  But peaceful ever be;
A foretaste sweet
Of bliss complete,
  Lasting eternally.

(*Source unverified*)

THESE words spake Jesus, and lifted up his eyes to heaven, and said, Father, the hour is come; glorify thy Son, that thy Son also may glorify thee:

As thou hast given him power over all flesh, that he should give eternal life to as many as thou hast given him.

And this is life eternal, that they might know thee the only true God, and Jesus Christ, whom thou hast sent.

I have glorified thee on the earth: I have finished the work which thou gavest me to do.

And now, O Father, glorify thou me with thine own self with the glory which I had with thee before the world was.

I have manifested thy name unto the men which thou gavest me out of the world: thine they were, and thou gavest them me; and they have kept thy word.

Now they have known that all things whatsoever thou hast given me are of thee.

For I have given unto them the words which thou gavest me; and they have received them, and have known surely that I came out from thee, and they have believed that thou didst send me.

I pray for them: I pray not for the world, but for them which thou hast given me; for they are thine.

And all mine are thine, and thine are mine; and I am glorified in them.

And now I am no more in the world, but these are in the world, and I come to thee. Holy Father, keep through thine own name those whom thou hast given me, that they may be one, as we are.

While I was with them in the world, I kept them in thy name: those that thou gavest me I have kept, and none of them is lost, but the son of perdition; that the scripture might be fulfilled.

And now come I to thee; and these things I speak in the world, that they might have my joy fulfilled in themselves.

I have given them thy word; and the world hath hated them, because they are not of the world, even as I am not of the world.

I pray not that thou shouldest take them out of the world, but that thou shouldest keep them from the evil.

They are not of the world, even as I am not of the world.

Sanctify them through thy truth: thy word is truth.

As thou hast sent me into the world, even so have I also sent them into the world.

And for their sakes I sanctify myself, that they also might be sanctified through the truth.

Neither pray I for these alone, but for them also which shall believe on me through their word;

That they all may be one; as thou, Father, art in me, and I in thee, that they also may be one in us: that the world may believe that thou hast sent me.

And the glory which thou gavest me I have given them; that they may be one, even as we are one:

I in them, and thou in me, that they may be made perfect in one; and that the world may know that thou hast sent me, and hast loved them, as thou hast loved me.

Father, I will that they also, whom thou hast given me, be with me where I am; that they may behold my glory, which thou hast given me: for thou lovedst me before the foundation of the world.

O righteous Father, the world hath not known thee: but I have known thee, and these have known that thou hast sent me.

And I have declared unto them thy name, and will declare it: that the love wherewith thou hast loved me may be in them, and I in them.

(*John* 17)

An Intercession

GRANT us peace, and establish Thy truth in us, as Thou fillest all things living with plenteousness. Remember every faithful soul in trial, and comfort, if it be possible, everyone in sorrow and distress. O Helper of the helpless, bring the wanderer home, and give health to the sick, and deliverance to the captive. Sustain the aged, comfort the weak-hearted, set free those whose souls are bound in misery and iron; remember all those who are in affliction, necessity, and emergency everywhere. Let us dwell with Thee in peace, as children of light, and in Thy light, Lord, let us see the light.

Direct, O Lord, in peace, the close of our life, trustfully, fearlessly, and, if it be Thy will, painlessly. Gather us when Thou wilt, into the abode of Thy chosen, without shame, or stain, or sin; for the sake of Jesus Christ Thy Son our Lord. AMEN.

ROWLAND WILLIAMS (1817–1870)

For the Special Needs of Some Among Us

O GOD, our help in ages past, our hope for years to come, in whom we live and move and have our being . . . teach us to set our trust in Thy gracious and abiding will. When we may not hold Thee fast or feel Thee near, help us to believe that Thou holdest us and all is well. We ask it in the faith of him who in the midst of the uncertainties of life found a will to hold him true, the same Jesus Christ our Lord. AMEN.

D. B. A.

For the Whole State of Christ's Church

ALMIGHTY and everliving God, Who by Thy holy Apostle hast taught us to make prayers, and supplications, and to give thanks for all men; We humbly beseech Thee most mercifully to accept our oblations, and to receive these our prayers, which we offer unto Thy Divine Majesty; beseeching Thee to inspire continually the Universal Church with the spirit of truth, unity, and concord: And grant that all those who do confess Thy holy Name may agree in the truth of Thy holy Word, and live in unity and godly love.

We beseech Thee also, so to direct and dispose the hearts of all Christian Rulers, that they may truly and impartially administer justice, to the punishment of wickedness and vice, and to the maintenance of Thy true religion, and virtue.

Give grace, O heavenly Father, to all Bishops and other Ministers, that they may, both by their life and doctrine, set forth Thy true and lively Word, and rightly and duly administer Thy holy Sacraments.

And to all Thy People give Thy heavenly grace; and especially to this congregation here present; that, with meek heart and due reverence, they may hear, and receive Thy holy Word; truly serving Thee in holiness and righteousness all the days of their life.

And we most humbly beseech Thee, of Thy goodness, O Lord, to comfort and succour all those who, in this transitory life, are in trouble, sorrow, need, sickness, or any other adversity.

And we also bless Thy holy Name for all Thy servants departed this life in Thy faith and fear; beseeching Thee to grant them continual growth in Thy love and service, and to give us grace so to follow their good examples, that with them we may be partakers of Thy heavenly kingdom. Grant this, O Father, for Jesus Christ's sake, our only Mediator and Advocate. AMEN.

(*The Book of Common Prayer*)

Oliver Cromwell's Last Prayer

LORD, though I am a miserable and wretched creature, I am in Covenant with Thee through grace. And I may, I will, come to Thee, for Thy People. Thou hast made me, though very unworthy, a mean instrument to do them some good, and Thee service; and many of them have set too high a value upon me, though others wish and would be glad of my death; Lord, however Thou dost dispose of me, continue and go on to do good for them. Give them consistency of judgment, one heart, and mutual love; and go on to deliver them, and with the work of reformation; and make the Name of Christ glorious in the world. Teach those who look too much on Thy instruments, to depend more upon Thyself. Pardon such as desire to trample upon the dust of a poor worm, for they are Thy People too. And pardon the folly of this short Prayer:—even for Jesus Christ's sake. And give us a good night, if it be Thy pleasure. AMEN.

OLIVER CROMWELL (1599–1658)

The Prayer of St. Stephen

AND he kneeled down, and cried with a loud voice, Lord, lay not this sin to their charge. And when he had said this, he fell asleep.

(*Acts* VII:60)

An Elizabethan Prayer for the Enemy

MOST merciful and loving Father,
We beseech Thee most humbly, even with all
    our hearts,
To pour out upon our enemies with bounti-

ful hands whatsoever things Thou knowest may do them good.
And chiefly a sound and uncorrupt mind,
Whereby they may know Thee and love Thee in true charity and with their whole heart.
And love us, Thy children, for Thy sake.
Let not their first hating of us turn to their harm
Seeing that we cannot do them good for want of ability,
Lord, we desire their amendment and our own.
Separate them not from us by punishing them,
But join and knit them to us by Thy favourable dealing with them,
And seeing we be all ordained to be citizens of the one everlasting City,
Let us begin to enter into that way here already by mutual love, which may bring us right-forth thither.

(*Source unverified*)

Dinah's Prayer for Hetty

JESUS, thou present Saviour! Thou hast known the depths of all sorrow, thou hast entered that black darkness where God is not, and has uttered the cry of the forsaken. Come, Lord, and gather the fruits of the travail and thy pleading; stretch forth thy hand, thou who art mighty to save to the uttermost, and rescue this lost one. She is clothed round with thick darkness; the fetters of her sin are upon her, and she cannot stir to come to thee: she can only feel her heart is hard, and she is helpless. She cries to me, thy weak creature . . . Saviour! It is a blind cry to thee. Hear it! Pierce the darkness! Look upon her with thy face of love and sorrow, that thou didst turn on him who denied thee, and melt her hard heart.

See, Lord,—I bring her, as they of old brought the sick and helpless, and thou didst heal them; I bear her on my arms and carry her before thee. Fear and trembling have taken hold on her; but she trembles only at the pain and death of the body; breathe upon her thy life-giving Spirit, and put a new fear within her,—the fear of her sin. Make her dread to keep the accursed thing within her soul: make her feel the presence of the living God, who beholds all the past, to whom the darkness is as noonday; who is waiting now, at the eleventh hour, for her to turn to him and confess her sin, and cry for mercy,—now before the night of death comes, and the moment of pardon is forever fled, like yesterday that returneth not.

Saviour! It is yet time,—time to snatch this poor soul from everlasting darkness. I believe—I believe in thy infinite love. What is *my* love or *my* pleading? It is quenched in thine. I can only clasp her in my weak arms, and urge her with my weak pity. Thou—thou wilt breathe on the dead soul, and it shall arise from the unanswering sleep of death.

Yea, Lord, I see thee coming through the darkness, coming like the morning with healing on thy wings. The marks of thy agony are upon thee,—I see, I see thou art able and willing to save,—thou wilt not let her perish forever. Come, mighty Saviour! Let the dead hear thy voice; let the eyes of the blind be opened. Let her see that God encompasses her; let her tremble at nothing but at the sin that cuts her off from him. Melt the hard heart; unseal the closed lips. Make her cry with her whole soul, "Father, I have sinned—"

George Eliot (1819–1880)

" 'Dinah,' Hetty sobbed out, throwing her arms round Dinah's neck, 'I will speak . . . I will tell . . . I won't hide it any more.' " This prayer and its prompt result are taken from Chapter X of Adam Bede. *Hetty had been imprisoned on the charge of murder-*

ing her baby and, says George Eliot, "Dinah held the clinging hand and all her soul went forth in her voice" as she prayed.

For Manual Workers and Others

O GOD, our Heavenly Father, we beseech Thee to hear us on behalf of all those who live by strength of arm or skill of hand. For men who face peril. For women who suffer pain. For those who till the earth; for those who tend machinery. For those whose business is in the deep waters, for sailors and seafarers. For those who work in offices and warehouses, for those who buy and sell. For those who labour at furnaces and in factories. For those who toil in mines. For those who keep house, for those who train children. For all who control, rule, or employ. For all who are poor, and broken and oppressed. For all whose labour is without hope; for all whose labour is without honour. For all whose labour is without interest. For those who have too little leisure. For those who are underpaid. We pray for all women-workers. We pray for all those who work in dangerous trades. For those who cannot find work, for those who have no home. For all prisoners and outcasts. For all who are sick, hungry, or destitute. We pray, O Father, for all men everywhere, that it may please Thee to comfort, sustain, protect, and support these, and all others for whom we desire to pray, through Jesus Christ our Lord. AMEN.

P. DEARMER (*twentieth century*)

For the Departed

O GOD, the God of the spirits of all flesh, in whose embrace all creatures live, in whatsoever world or condition they be; I beseech Thee for him whose name and dwelling place and every need Thou knowest. Lord, vouchsafe him light and rest, peace, refreshment, joy and consolation, in paradise, in the companionship of saints, in the presence of Christ, in the ample folds of Thy great love.

If in aught I can minister to his peace be pleased of Thy love to let this be; and mercifully keep me from every act which may deprive me of the sight of him as soon as our trial time is over; or mar the fullness of our joy when the end of days hath come; through Jesus Christ our Lord. AMEN.

WILLIAM EWART GLADSTONE
(1809–1898)

"*Abe Lincoln in Illinois*"

ABE (*taking off his hat*)—Oh, God, the Father of all living, I ask You to look with gentle mercy upon this little boy who is here, lying sick in this covered wagon. His people are traveling far, to seek a new home in the wilderness, to do Your work, God, to make this earth a good place for Your children to live in. They can see clearly where they're going, and they're not afraid to face all the perils that lie along the way. I humbly beg You not to take their child from them. Grant him the freedom of life. Do not condemn him to the imprisonment of death. Do not deny him his birthright. Let him know the sight of great plains and high mountains, of green valleys and wide rivers. For this little boy is an American, and these things belong to him, and he to them. Spare him, that he too may strive for the ideal for which his fathers have labored, so faithfully and for so long. Spare him and give him his father's strength—give us all strength, O God, to do the work that is before us. I ask You this favor, in the name of Your Son, Jesus Christ, who died upon the Cross to set men free. AMEN.

ROBERT E. SHERWOOD (1938)

The preceding prayer is from Abe Lincoln in Illinois, *a drama in three acts, with Raymond Massey in the part of Lincoln.*

The scene is in the second act. Seth Gale, an old acquaintance of Lincoln's, with his wife, Aggie, and little Jimmy, are camped with their open wagon on the prairie near New Salem. The boy has been ill with swamp fever, and suddenly takes a turn for the worse. Abe says, "If you wish me to, Mrs. Gale, I'll try to speak a prayer." "We'd be grateful for anything you might say, Abe," Seth replies.

A Prayer of St. Chrysostom

ALMIGHTY God, Who hast given us grace at this time with one accord to make our common supplications unto Thee; and dost promise that when two or three are gathered together in Thy Name Thou wilt grant their requests; Fulfil now, O Lord, the desires and petitions of Thy servants, as may be most expedient for them; granting us in this world knowledge of Thy truth, and in the world to come life everlasting. AMEN.

(*The Book of Common Prayer*)

X. FOR SPECIAL OCCASIONS

X. FOR SPECIAL OCCASIONS

A. COUNTRY

I MUST die with malice and hatred in my heart toward no one.

EDITH CAVELL

For our Country

ALMIGHTY God, who hast given us this good land for our heritage; We humbly beseech thee that we may always prove ourselves a people mindful of thy favour and glad to do thy will. Bless our land with honourable industry, sound learning, and pure manners. Save us from violence, discord, and confusion; from pride and arrogancy, and from every evil way. Defend our liberties, and fashion into one united people the multitudes brought hither out of many kindreds and tongues. Endue with the spirit of wisdom those to whom in thy Name we entrust the authority of government, that there may be justice and peace at home, and that, through obedience to thy law, we may show forth thy praise among the nations of the earth. In the time of prosperity, fill our hearts with thankfulness, and in the day of trouble, suffer not our trust in thee to fail; all which we ask through Jesus Christ our Lord. AMEN.

(*The Book of Common Prayer*)

A Prayer for Our Country

O ALMIGHTY God, Judge of the nations, in honest self-searching we know our ways have not been thy ways, O thou most just and true. On the roll of the centuries, we have oft cloaked national gain in the garb of honor; confused greatness with political power; ignored injustice and poverty within our own gates; made terms of conquest which precluded a lasting peace.

God the All-merciful! earth hath forsaken
Thy ways of blessedness, slighted thy word.

Yet in thy mercy—forgive.

Let us stand, O God, for the Right, and help us to restore. Where the sacredness of the sealed word has been broken; where wanton cruelty has held sway; where liberty and the free choice denied, and the sanctity of thy Spirit scorned, help us to stand, and having done all, to stand. Strengthen us to make no compromise with oppression or to our seeming advantage come to terms with the evil. Give us an abiding hatred of wrong which we oppose and a generous forgiveness to the doer, lest our own trespasses be unforgiven in thy sight.

God the All-righteous One! man hath defied thee;
Yet to eternity standeth thy word,
Falsehood and wrong shall not tarry beside thee;
Give to us peace in our time, O Lord. AMEN.

D. B. A.

ALMIGHTY God, in whose truth is no uncertainty, we acknowledge, when our fragment of Thy work is done, that our times are in Thy hand. Out of the night we trust, with deathless faith, that what is real in Thee will show the unreal in our human ways and make it one with Nineveh and Tyre.

Before Thy judgment seat we stand with all free peoples of

the world, for we have in part betrayed Thy trust and are learning where the grapes of wrath are stored. We pray for all of us the burning zeal of a humble and a contrite heart, to set our wills against the thirst for vengeance, the dreary round of hate returned, the devil's promise of dominion over men, and all vain boastings of the lust for power by which we can be corrupted and deceived.

Once more make us worthy, one by one, of this land of the oppressed where our exiled fathers and all the breeds of earth came flocking to be free, and let no safe prosperity be our portion with those who have feared not blood nor sweat nor tears.

Let thine ancient cross upon its lonely hill illumine all our calvaries, while we join hands across the borders and the seas to clear the air of lies, to enlist our common hopes against our separate fears, and with all our skills combined, rebuild upon the ruins a new and ampler home for man's spirit in all the corners of the earth.

DEAN ROBERT R. WICKS

OUR fathers' God! to Thee,
   Author of liberty,
   To Thee we sing:
Long may our land be bright
With freedom's holy light;
Protect us by Thy might,
   Great God, our King!

S. F. SMITH, *America.*

This popular national anthem was composed on an afternoon in February, 1832. The author was a Baptist minister. While glancing through a music book, he came upon the British "God Save the King" and felt the impulse to write a patriotic hymn for America. "Picking up a scrap of waste paper which lay near me," he said afterward, "I wrote at once, probably within half an hour, the hymn 'America' as it is now known everywhere." He gave the manuscript to Lowell Mason, the music composer. Mason made it public for the first time at a children's celebration on the following Fourth of July at the Park Street Church in Boston.

For Our Country

O GOD, our Ruler, give to every State a deeper sense of human brotherhood, a new respect for man and reverence for woman, new loyalty in service, compunction and charity, new happiness in work and justice in reward; that our homes may be restored in Thee, our cities rebuilt, and all the world may reflect the radiance of the Throne which is eternal in the heavens. AMEN.

(*Source unverified*)

A *Prayer for Congress*

MOST gracious God, we humbly beseech Thee, as for the people of these United States in general, so especially for their Senate and Representatives in Congress assembled; that Thou wouldest be pleased to direct and prosper all their consultations, to the advancement of Thy glory, the good of Thy Church, the safety, honour, and welfare of Thy people; that all things may be so ordered and settled by their endeavours, upon the best and surest foundations, that peace and happiness, truth and justice, religion and piety, may be established among us for all generations. These and all other necessaries, for them, for us, and Thy whole Church, we humbly beg in the Name and meditation of Jesus Christ, our most blessed Lord and Saviour. AMEN.

(*The Book of Common Prayer*)

West Point Cadet Prayer

O GOD, our Father, Thou Searcher of men's hearts, help us to draw near to Thee in sincerity and truth. May our religion be filled with gladness and may our worship of Thee be natural.

Strengthen and increase our admiration for honest dealing and clean thinking, and suffer not our hatred of hypocrisy and pretence ever to diminish. Encourage us in our endeavor to live above the common level of life. Make us to choose the harder right instead of the easier wrong, and never to be content with a half truth when the whole can be won. Endow us with courage that is born of loyalty to all that is noble and worthy, that scorns compromise with vice and injustice and knows no fear when truth and right are in jeopardy. Guard us against flippancy and irreverence in the sacred things of life. Grant us new ties of friendship and new opportunities of service. Kindle our hearts in fellowship with those of a cheerful countenance, and soften our hearts with sympathy for those who sorrow and suffer. May we find genuine pleasure in clean and wholesome mirth and feel inherent disgust for all coarse-minded humor. Help us, in our work and in our play, to keep ourselves physically strong, mentally awake and morally straight. All of which we ask in the name of the Great Friend and Master of men. AMEN.

For Unity

ALMIGHTY God, grant unto us, we beseech Thee, a succession of rulers learned in the wisdom of the kingdom of Christ. Endue our law-givers with a right understanding and a pure purpose; enable them to rise above all self-seeking and party zeal into the larger desire for public good and human brotherhood. Purge our public life of evil, subdue in the nation all thirst for conquest and vain-glory, and inspire us with calmness and self-restraint, to Thy honour and glory, Who ever liveth and reigneth, one God world without end. AMEN.

(*Source unverified*)

For Right Judgment on Election Day

O ETERNAL God whose overruling spirit can shape the destinies of Nations and of men, guide, we beseech Thee, the decision of the people of these United States as they choose who shall lead them. Dispel from our hearts all prejudice and self-seeking, all expediency and half-truth. Help us to see where wisdom and vision and manhood lie, that such may speak in dignity in the high office of President of this land. Let us make this nation, not the master but the servant of the nations of the earth—leading the world for Thee, whose service is perfect freedom. Thy love divine hath led us in the past. In this free land by Thee our lot is cast. Be Thou our ruler, guardian, guide and stay. Thy word our law, Thy paths our chosen way. AMEN.

D. B. A.

Airmen's Hymn

GOD of the shining hosts that range on high,
Lord of the Seraphs serving day and night,
Hear us for these, our squadrons of the sky,
And give to them the shelter of Thy might.

Thine are the arrows of the storm cloud's breath,
Thine, too, the tempest or the zephyr still;
Take in Thy keeping those who, facing death,
Bravely go forth to do a nation's will.

High in the trackless space that paves Thy throne,
Claim by Thy love these souls in danger's thrall;
Be Thou their Pilot through the great unknown,
Then shall they mount as eagles and not fall.

The Air Force

LOOK in Thy mercy, we beseech Thee, O Lord, on those who are called to tasks of special peril, in the air or beneath the sea. Even there also shall Thy hand lead them, and Thy right hand shall hold them. Help them to do their duty with prudence and with fearlessness, confident that in life or in death the Eternal God is their refuge, and underneath them are the Everlasting Arms. Grant this, for Jesus Christ's sake, thy Son our Lord. AMEN.

RANDALL DAVIDSON, ARCHBISHOP OF CANTERBURY (1915)

The Air Force

AS on unseen pinions, bear
Our devoted men who dare
All the perils of the air.
Keep them, we beseech Thee.

F. W. S. (1915)

For Those in Industry

O LORD, Who in the gift of Thine only Son hast encouraged struggling mankind, grant that the labor movement may be wisely guided into a greater vision of usefulness, that employers of labor may fashion their dealings according to justice, and that the way of those in industry may lead to that Kingdom toward which Thou hast pointed us, through Jesus Christ, our Lord. AMEN.

GOD of our fathers, Whose almighty hand
Leads forth in beauty all the starry band
Of shining worlds in splendor through the skies,
Our grateful songs before Thy throne arise.

Thy love divine hath led us in the past,
In this free land by Thee our lot is cast;
Be Thou our ruler, guardian, guide and stay,
Thy word our law, Thy paths our chosen way.

From war's alarms, from deadly pestilence,
Be Thy strong arm our ever sure defense;
Thy true religion in our hearts increase,
Thy bounteous goodness nourish us in peace.

Refresh Thy people on their toilsome way,
Lead us from night to never-ending day;
Fill all our lives with love and grace divine,
And glory, laud and praise be ever Thine.

DANIEL C. ROBERTS

B. CRISES

A Wartime Prayer

O GOD of all being, throned afar, by whose universal laws suns and stars move surely in their appointed ways, and by whose indwelling spirit men may, if they will, as surely dwell together in amity and accord—grant, we beseech Thee, to men everywhere Thy will to Peace. Remove from our minds all malice and prejudice born of past battles and by-gone wars. Free us from impatience for power and the greed of gain. Restrain us from all vain boasting and that provincial conceit which remoteness can create. And if we must arm, may this strength be used but to police and preserve the world's needed peace. Mercifully grant that the free-will Thou hast given to all men may be turned away from that which destroys to that which saves. We ask it in the name of the Prince of Peace, our Saviour. AMEN.

D. B. A.

In Times of National Anxiety

GRANT calmness and control of thought to those who are facing uncertainty and anxiety: let their hearts stand fast, believing in the Lord.

Be Thou all things to all men, knowing each one and his petition, each house and its need, for the sake of Jesus Christ. AMEN.

(*Russian Liturgy*)

O ALMIGHTY and everlasting God! How terrible is this world! Behold it openeth its mouth to swallow me up, and I have so little trust in Thee! How weak is the flesh and how powerful is Satan! If it is in the strength of this world only that I must put my trust, all is over! My last hour is come, my condemnation has been pronounced. O God! O God! O God! Do Thou help me against all the wisdom of the world! Do this; Thou shouldst do this; Thou alone, for this is not my work but Thine! I have nothing to do here, nothing to contend for with these great ones of the world! I should desire to see my days flow on peaceful and happy. But the cause is Thine, and it is a righteous and eternal cause. O Lord! Help me! Faithful and unchangeable God! In no man do I place my trust. It would be vain—all that is of man is uncertain, all that cometh of man fails. O God! My God, hearest Thou me not? My God, art Thou dead? No! No, Thou canst not die! Thou hidest Thyself only! Thou hast chosen me for this work. I know it well! Act then, O God, stand at my side, for the sake of Thy well-beloved Son, Jesus Christ, who is my defense, my shield, and my strong tower.

Lord, where stayest Thou! O my God, where art Thou? Come! Come! I am ready to lay down my life for Thy truth, patient as a lamb. For it is the cause of justice—it is Thine! I will never separate myself from Thee, neither now nor through eternity! And though the world may be filled with devils, though my body, which is still the work of Thy hands, should be slain, be stretched upon the pavement, be cut in pieces, reduced to ashes—my soul is Thine! Yes, I have the assurance of Thy word. My soul belongs to Thee! It shall abide forever with Thee. AMEN. O God! Help me! AMEN.

MARTIN LUTHER (1483–1546)

Prayer of Martin Luther on April 18, 1521, the day when he was brought before the Diet at Worms. On the evening of the same day, in the midst of the great assembly, he declared, "I cannot and I will not retract. Here I stand, I can do no other. May God help me! AMEN."

TAKE from us, O God, all pride and vanity, all boasting and forwardness, and give us the true courage that shows itself by gentleness; the true wisdom that shows itself by simplicity; and the true power that shows itself by modesty; through Jesus Christ our Lord. AMEN.

CHARLES KINGSLEY (1819–1875)

LORD, we pray not for tranquillity, nor that our tribulations may cease; we pray for Thy Spirit and Thy Love, that Thou grant us strength and grace to overcome adversity; through Jesus Christ. AMEN.

GIROLAMO SAVONAROLA (1452–1498)

Girolamo Savonarola, a Florentine resembling an Old Testament prophet, preached that the Kingdom of God might come to earth. A Church and State controlled by custom and so-called common sense failed to understand him and brought him to the stake.

Before Going into Battle

LORD, I shall be verie busie this day:
I may forget Thee, but doe Thou not forget me!

GENERAL SIR JACOB ASTLEY
(1579–1652)

Prayer before the Battle of Edgehill, the first battle of England's civil war. Astley was on the Royalist side.

A Wartime Prayer

AS the lights of peace again go out in Europe, we reaffirm our faith in the ultimate triumph of good over evil, truth over error, light over darkness. Have mercy we pray Thee, O Lord, on the souls of those who have died and are dying in battle, and succor the great army of refugees who wander, homeless and forsaken, in every corner of Europe. Re-establish, we beseech Thee, the principles of justice, mercy, and truth by which men may, if they will, live together in peace and security. And if it be Thy will, grant to the warring nations an early truce and an enduring peace. We ask it in the name of Him who died that men might live, our Savior, Jesus Christ. AMEN.

J. B. H.

A Wartime Prayer

BE Merciful, O God, unto all who need Thy mercy, and let the angel of Thy presence save the afflicted, the exiled and imprisoned; be Thou the strength of the weary, the comfort of the sorrowful, the friend of the desolate, the light of the wandering, the hope of the dying, the Saviour of the lost, for Jesus' sake. AMEN.

(*War-Time Prayers*)

Prayer of a Soldier in France

MY shoulders ache beneath my pack;
(Lie easier, Cross, upon His back).

I march with feet that burn and smart;
(Tread, Holy Feet, upon my heart).

Men shout at me that may not speak;
(They scourged Thy back and smote Thy cheek).

I may not lift a hand to clear
My eyes of salty drops that sear.

(Then shall my guilty soul forget
Thy agony of Bloody Sweat?)

Lord, Thou didst suffer more for me
Than all the hosts of land and sea.
So let me render back again
This millionth of Thy gift. AMEN.

(JOYCE KILMER)

A Wartime Prayer

ALMIGHTY God, grant me thy gift of loyalty. For my home give me love and obedience; for my country, sacrifice and service; for my Church, reverence and devotion; and in everything make me true to thee; through thy Son, our Saviour, Jesus Christ. AMEN.

(*Source unverified*)

A Wartime Prayer

O GOD, our help in ages past, our hope today and forever, have mercy upon humanity in its blindness, its bitterness, and its confusion. Deliver us, O Lord, from lust of power, from vanity of spirit, from envy, apathy, and ill-will. Touch our minds with light, that, having a right understanding, we may have compassion, and courage, and patience—working with Thy help for the better order of the ages. In the name of Jesus Christ our Lord. AMEN.

(*Source unverified*)

A Wartime Prayer

O GOD, who knowest all things in earth and heaven, so fill my heart with trust in thee, that by night and by day, at all times and in all seasons, I may, without fear, commit those who are dear to me to thy never-failing love, for this life and the life to come. AMEN.

(*Source unverified*)

Wartime Prayer

TEACH us, O Lord, to check in ourselves and in others every temper which makes for war, all ungenerous judgments, all promptings of self-assertion, all presumptuous claims; that being ever ready to recognize the needs and aspirations of other nations, we may, with patience, do whatsoever in us lies to remove suspicions and misunderstandings; and to honor all men in Jesus Christ our Lord. AMEN.

(*War-Time Prayers*)

From the Prayers Used at the Church Service Held Sunday Morning, 10 August, 1941, on the Quarter-Deck of the H.M.S. "Prince of Wales," at Sea, and Attended by Franklin D. Roosevelt, President of the United States, and the Prime Minister of Great Britain, Winston S. Churchill

Let us pray for the invading countries, in the grief and havoc of oppression for the upholding of their courage and hope for the speedy restoration of their freedom.

O LORD God, whose compassions fail not, support, we entreat Thee, the peoples on whom the terrors of invasion have fallen; and if their liberty be lost to the oppressor, let not this spirit and hope be broken, but stayed upon Thy strength till the day of deliverance. Through Jesus Christ our Lord. AMEN.

Let us pray for all who suffer by reason of the War, for the Sick and Wounded, for Prisoners, for the exiled and homeless, for the anxious and bereaved.

WE bring before Thee, O Lord, the griefs and perils of peoples and nations; the sighing of prisoners; the necessities of the homeless, the helplessness of the weak; the pains of the sick and wounded; the sorrows of the bereaved. Comfort and relieve them, O Merciful Father, according to their several needs, for the sake of Thy Son, our Saviour and Christ. AMEN.

O GOD, the righteous Judge strong and patient, who by the words and wounds of Thy dear Son has bidden us pray for them that despitefully use us; we beseech Thee so to turn the hearts of our enemies that, when this tyranny be overpast, the divisions of all peoples may be healed, in the bond and by the blessing of the same, our Lord and Saviour Jesus Christ. AMEN.

Prayer for Our Friends and Families.

O LORD, our Heavenly Father, who hast bestowed upon us the blessings of friends and families, look down in love upon our kindred. Protect and keep them from all harm; prosper and bless them in all things good; suffer them never to be lonely, unhappy, nor troubled; let no shadow come between them and us to divide our hearts; and in Thine own good time bring us home to them again. Through the same Thy Son Jesus Christ our Lord. AMEN.

STABLISH our hearts, O God, in the day of battle, and strengthen our resolve, that we fight, not in enmity against men, but against the powers of darkness enslaving the souls of men; till all enmity and oppression be done away, and the peoples of the world be set free from fear to serve one another; as children of our Father, who is above all and through all and in all, our God for ever and ever. AMEN.

O ETERNAL Lord God, who alone spreadest out the heavens, and rulest the raging of the seas; who hast compassed the waters with bounds until day and night come to an end; be pleased to receive into Thy Almighty and most Gracious protection the persons of us Thy servants of the Fleet in which we serve. Preserve us from the dangers of the sea and from the violence of the enemy; that we may be a security for such as pass on the seas upon their lawful occasions; that the peoples of the empire may in peace and quietness serve Thee our God; and that we may return in safety to enjoy the blessings of the Lord. With the fruits of our labours and with a thankful remembrance of Thy mercies to praise and glorify Thy Holy Name; through Jesus Christ our Lord. AMEN.

ALMIGHTY God, the fountain of all wisdom, who knowest our necessities before we ask, and our ignorance in asking: We beseech Thee to have compassion upon our infirmities; and those things, which for our unworthiness we dare not, and for our blindness we cannot ask, vouchsafe to give us, for the worthiness of Thy Son Jesus Christ our Lord. AMEN.

(Used by special permission of the President of the United States)

For Forgiveness and the Will for Peace

QUICKEN our consciences, O God, to feel the sin and shame of war. Inspire us with faith and courage to lift up our voices against private greed, social injustice, the aggression of the strong against the weak, and whatsoever else works enmity between man and man, class and class, nation and nation. Create within us a passion for the reign of righteousness, good will and brotherhood, and so fulfill Thine ancient word, "Nation shall not lift up sword against nation, neither shall they learn war any more"; through Jesus Christ our Lord. AMEN.

(War-Time Prayers)

C. PEACE

For Peace in the World

O GOD, the physician of men and nations, the restorer of the years that have been destroyed; look upon the distractions of the world, and be pleased to complete the work of Thy healing hand; draw all men unto Thee and one to another by the bands of Thy love; make Thy Church one, and fill it with Thy Spirit, that by Thy power it may unite the world in a sacred brotherhood of nations, wherein justice, mercy and faith, truth and freedom may flourish, and Thou mayest be ever glorified; through Jesus Christ our Lord. AMEN.

(Acts of Devotion)

Prayer for World Peace

DISMAYED by the strife and jealousy which are bringing ruin to peoples and nations, we turn, O Jesus, to Thy most loving Heart as our only hope. O God of mercy, with tears we invoke Thee to end wars and the horror of war. O King of Peace, we humbly implore the peace for which we long.

From Thy Sacred Heart Thou didst shed forth over the world divine charity, so that discord might end and love alone might reign among men. During Thy life on earth, Thy heart beat with tender compassion for the sorrows of men. In this day, when hate often dominates, may Thy divine Heart be once more moved to pity.

Inspire rulers and peoples with counsels of meekness. Heal the discords that tear nations asunder. Thou Who didst shed Thy precious blood that they might live as brothers, bring men together once more in loving harmony. To the cry of the Apostle Peter: "Save us, Lord, we perish," Thou didst answer words of mercy and didst still the raging waves. Deign now to hear our trustful prayers and give back to the world order and peace.

And do thou, O most Holy Virgin, as in other times of distress, be our help, our protection, and our safeguard. AMEN.

BENEDICT XV (1854–1922)

Prayers for Peace

COMMUNION PRAYER

O LORD Jesus Christ, Who didst say to Thy Apostles, Peace I leave with you, My peace I give unto you; look not upon my sins, but upon the faith of Thy Church; and vouchsafe to Her that peace and unity which is agreeable to Thy Will; Who livest and reignest God forever and ever. AMEN.

O GOD, Who sufferest not the nations who believe in Thee to be overwhelmed by any peril; vouchsafe to receive the prayers and offerings of Thy people, that in Thy mercy Thou wouldst grant peace to Christendom and make it secure against all its enemies. Through our Lord Jesus Christ Thy Son, Who liveth and reigneth with Thee in the unity of the Holy Ghost, God forever and ever. AMEN.

(*The Mass for Peace*, ROMAN MISSAL)

Peace

O GOD our Father, on this Day of Remembrance, look upon the unrest of the world and be pleased to complete the work of Thy healing hand. Send peace upon the earth, a deeper and more lasting peace than the world has ever known. Draw all men unto Thyself, and to one another by the bands of love. Grant understanding to the Nations with an increase of sympathy and mutual good will, that they may be united in a sacred Brotherhood wherein justice, mercy and faith, truth and freedom may flourish, so that the sacrifice of those who died may not have been made in vain, for the sake of Christ Jesus our Lord. AMEN.

(*A Chain of Prayers across the Ages*)

The Land

O LORD of splendid nations, let us dream
Not of a place of barter, nor "the State,"
But dream as lovers dream—for it is late—
Of some small place beloved; perhaps a stream
Running beside a house set round with flowers;
Perhaps a garden wet with hurrying showers,
Where bees are thick about a leaf-hid gate.
For such as these, men die nor hesitate.
The old gray cities, gossipy and wise,
The candid valleys, like a woman's brow,
The mountains treading mightily toward the skies,
Turn dreams to visions—there's a vision now!
Of hills panoplied, fields of waving spears,
And a great campus shaken with flags and tears.

MAXWELL STRUTHERS BURT

Our Shelter Prayer

INCREASE, O God, the spirit of neighborliness among us, that in peril we may uphold one another, in calamity serve one another, in suffering tend one another, and in homelessness, loneliness or exile befriend one another. Grant us brave and enduring hearts that we may strengthen one another, till the disciplines and testing of these days be ended, and Thou dost give again peace in our time. Through Jesus Christ, our Lord. AMEN.

Those who frequent the air-raid shelters in Hull, Birmingham and Westminster (England) are making wide use of this prayer.

Recessional

God of our fathers, known of old—
Lord of our far-flung battle line—
Beneath whose awful hand we hold
Dominion over palm and pine—
Lord God of Hosts, be with us yet,
Lest we forget—lest we forget!

The tumult and the shouting dies—
The Captains and the Kings depart—
Still stands Thine ancient sacrifice,
An humble and a contrite heart.
Lord God of Hosts, be with us yet,
Lest we forget—lest we forget!

Far-called, our navies melt away—
On dune and headland sinks the fire—
Lo, all our pomp of yesterday
Is one with Nineveh and Tyre!
Judge of the Nations, spare us yet,
Lest we forget—lest we forget!

If, drunk with sight of power, we loose
Wild tongues that have not Thee in awe—
Such boasting as the Gentiles use,
Or lesser breeds without the Law—
Lord God of Hosts, be with us yet,
Lest we forget—lest we forget!

For heathen heart that puts her trust
In reeking tube and iron shard—
All valiant dust that builds on dust,

And guarding calls not Thee to guard—
For frantic boast and foolish word,
Thy Mercy on Thy People, Lord!

AMEN

RUDYARD KIPLING (1865–1936)

This famous prayer-poem by Rudyard Kipling, written in 1897, was inspired by the Jubilee celebration of the sixtieth year of Queen Victoria's reign. The British Empire may be said then to have reached the pinnacle of its world power and prestige. In order to warn his fellow countrymen against undue pride and boasting, such as the national celebration tended to inspire, Kipling composed this "Recessional."

He sent the poem to the editor of the London Times *with a letter, in which he said, "Enclosed please find my sentiments on things—which I hope are yours. We've been blowing up the Trumpets of the New Moon a little too much for white men, and it's about time we sobered down. If you would like it, it's at your service—on the old conditions that I can use it if I want it later in book form. The sooner it's in print the better."*

The Recessional was published next day. The editor asked Kipling to name his own price for the poem, but the latter refused to accept any payment. The poem instantly sprang into world-wide popularity among English-speaking peoples.

A Seventeenth Century Prayer for England

IN Thy name, oh God, do we set up our banners. Go forth, therefore, with our fleets and armies, that through Thee we may do valiantly. And do Thou, oh Lord of Hosts, tread down our enemies. Plead our cause against an ungodly nation. Deliver us from that unjust man, the enemy and the oppressor. Let him no longer be able to vex the Lord's people with ambitious and unrighteous wars. . . . Arise, oh God, and scatter Thou this people that delight in war. . . . Let them be confounded and put to shame. . . . But bless and preserve all those that trust in Thee that, working righteousness, they may out of weakness be made strong, wax valiant in fight, turn to flight the armies of the aliens . . . and finally obtain Thy promises. In a most special manner, give Thy holy angels charge of our Sovereign Lord the King. . . . Let no weapon formed against him prosper. . . . Make him a terror to his foes abroad and cheerfully and gratefully obeyed at home. . . . And after Thou hast made him a glorious instrument of establishing peace and truth upon earth, let him long enjoy the fruits of his labors, and at last crown them with everlasting peace . . . with Thee in Thy kingdom. Bless also that excellent woman, the partner to his throne and cares. Let Thy Providence watch over her and Thy Holy Spirit direct and guide her. . . . Let her days be many and happy; and, if Thou see fit, let her children inherit her crown and virtues, when she herself shall be taken to reign with Thee and Thy saints in glory everlasting.

This prayer, drafted by Daniel, Earl of Nottingham, in his own hand and probably written between 1689 and 1696, was found at Burley, July, 1939, by W. Appleton Aiken.

A Prayer for the Homeland

O THOU, upon Whom the isles do wait, and in Whom is their trust, save this island and all the country in which we sojourn, from all affliction, peril, and necessity; for the sake of Jesus Christ. AMEN.

BISHOP LANCELOT ANDREWES (1555)

For Social Justice

ALMIGHTY God, Who hast created man in Thine own image; Grant us grace fearlessly to contend against evil, and to make no peace with oppression; and, that we may reverently use our freedom, help us to employ it in the maintenance of justice among men and nations, to the glory of Thy Holy Name; through Jesus Christ, our Lord. AMEN.

(*Prayers, New and Old*)

D. FOR THOSE IN SPECIAL NEED

ETERNAL Father! strong to save,
Whose arm hath bound the restless wave,
Who bidd'st the mighty ocean deep
Its own appointed limits keep;
  Oh, hear us when we cry to Thee
  For those in peril on the sea!

O Christ! Whose voice the waters heard
And hushed their raging at Thy word,
Who walked'st on the foaming deep,
And calm amidst its rage didst sleep;
  Oh, hear us when we cry to Thee
  For those in peril on the sea!

Most Holy Spirit! Who didst brood
Upon the chaos dark and rude,
And bid its angry tumult cease,
And give, for wild confusion, peace;
  Oh, hear us when we cry to Thee
  For those in peril on the sea!

O Trinity of love and power!
Our brethren shield in danger's hour;
From rock and tempest, fire and foe,
Protect them whersoe'er they go;
Thus evermore shall rise to Thee
Glad hymns of praise from land and sea.

WILLIAM WHITING

A Prayer for the Unemployed

ALMIGHTY God whose loving kindness faileth not, and whose mercy reacheth unto the end of the world, we beseech thee especially for the people of this land who are destitute or discouraged because they cannot find work. Save them, we beseech thee, from bitterness. Preserve them from despair in those hours when they feel that they are not needed by their fellowmen. Encourage them with the knowledge of thy never-failing love and with the fellowship of thy days of poverty on earth.

But particularly we beseech thee, most merciful Lord, to open not only the hearts of those whose bounty may relieve their material distresses, but also the minds and imaginations of all thy servants in places of responsibility, that they may be enabled to devise ways and means whereby the burden of financial depression may be lifted from those least able to bear it, and whereby all mankind may be admitted to a share in the toil and the rewards of useful industry.

This we ask in the Name of that Friend and Companion of the unfortunate, Thy Son our Saviour, Jesus Christ. AMEN.

B. A. STAMBAUGH

THOU God of Providence, grant to farmers and keepers of cattle good seasons; to the fleet and fishers fair weather; to tradesmen not to overreach one another; to mechanics to pursue their business lawfully, even down to the meanest workman, even down to the poor; for Christ's sake. AMEN.

BISHOP LANCELOT ANDREWES

For Service of Healing

ALMIGHTY God, who are the only source of health and healing, the spirit of calm and central peace of the universe: grant to us, Thy children, such a consciousness of Thy indwelling presence as may give us utter confidence in Thee. In all pain and weariness and anxiety may we throw ourselves upon Thy besetting care, that knowing ourselves fenced about by Thy loving omnipotence, we may permit Thee to give us health and strength and peace; through Jesus Christ our Lord. AMEN.

JAMES THAYER ADDISON

ALL-SEEING Light and Eternal Life of all things, look upon my misery with Thine eye of mercy, and let Thine infinite power vouchsafe to limit out some portion of deliverance unto me, as unto Thee shall seem most convenient. O my God, I yield unto Thy will, and joyfully embrace what sorrow Thou wilt have me suffer. Only this much let me crave of Thee—let me crave even by the noblest title, which is my greatest affliction I may give myself, that I am Thy creature, and by Thy goodness, that Thou wilt suffer some beam of Thy Majesty so to shine into my mind, that it may still depend confidentially on Thee. AMEN.

SIR PHILIP SIDNEY (1554–1586)

Sir Philip Sidney made a name for himself in the two unrelated fields of war and poetry, but he achieved fame as a man of letters. He was one of the knightliest of men. He fell mortally wounded at the Battle of Zutphen.

For Those in Mental Darkness

O, MOST merciful God, who art both the Mind of thy creation and the Father of us all, send thy light to thy children who grope in mental darkness and the dimness of uncertain sight. Turn the night of their distress into the morning of thy hope, and cause them and those who watch and wait to rest confidently in thee. We ask it in the name of Jesus Christ our Lord. AMEN.

D. B. A.

E. FOR THE CHURCH

Two Seventeenth Century Prayers

ALMIGHTY and everlasting God! who only workest great marvells, show the riches of Thy goodness to Thy desolate and persecuted church, that now sits mourning in her own dust and ruins, torn by schism and stripped and spoiled by sacrilege.

And Thou, who after a long captivity didst bring back Thy people to rebuild their Temple, look upon us with the same eyes of mercy.

Restore to us once again the publick worship of Thy name, the reverent administration of Thy sacraments; raise up the ——— * that we may once more enter into Thy courts with praise and serve Thee with that reverence, that unity, and order, as may be acceptable in Thy sight, through Jesus Xt our Lord. AMEN.

O MOST powerful and ever blessed Lord God! who art glorious in holiness, fearful in praises, doing wonders; we most humbly beseech Thee to look compassionately on this persecuted

* The King?

part of Thy church, now driven from Thy publick altars into corners and secret clossets, that Thy protection may be over us, wherever we shall be scattered, and a remnant preserved amongst us by whom Thy name may be glorified, Thy sacraments administered, and the souls of Thy servants kept upright in the midst of a corrupting and a corrupted generation. So we that are Thy people and sheep of Thy pasture shall give Thee thanks for ever, and will always be showing forth Thy praise from generation to generation, through Jesus Xt, our only Saviour and Redeemer. AMEN.

These prayers appeared in a James II prayer book of 1688, evidently composed by a priest of the Church of England for the King's own private devotions during the Commonwealth and copied by hand into his new prayer book in 1688. They have never before been published.

A Prayer for This Church

O GRACIOUS Father, we humbly beseech thee for this Thy Church; that Thou wouldst be pleased to fill it with all truth in all peace. Where it is corrupt, purify it; where it is in error, direct it; where in anything it is amiss, reform it. Where it is right, establish it; where it is in want, provide for it; for the sake of Him who died and rose again, and ever liveth to make intercession for it, Jesus Christ, thy Son, our Lord. AMEN.

(Adapted from *The Book of Common Prayer*)

LORD of our life, and God of our salvation,
Star of our night, and hope of every nation,
Hear and receive Thy Church's supplication,
Lord God Almighty.

See round Thine Ark the hungry billows curling!
See how Thy foes their banners are unfurling!
Lord, while their darts envenomed they are hurling,
Thou canst preserve us.

Lord, Thou canst help when earthly armor faileth;
Lord, Thou canst save when deadly sin assaileth;
Lord, o'er Thy Rock nor death nor hell prevaileth:
Grant us Thy peace, Lord!

Peace, in our hearts, our evil thoughts assuaging,
Peace, in Thy Church, where brothers are engaging,
Peace, when the world its busy war is waging;
Calm Thy foes raging!

Grant us Thy help till backward they are driven;
Grant them Thy truth, that they may be forgiven;
Grant peace on earth, and after we have striven,
Peace in Thy heaven.

PHILIP PUSEY. Translated from Löwenstern

For the Parish

ALMIGHTY and everlasting God, Who dost govern all things in heaven and earth: mercifully hear the supplications of us Thy servants, and grant unto this parish all things that are needful for its spiritual welfare. Strengthen and confirm the faithful; visit and relieve the sick and afflicted; turn and soften the wicked; rouse the careless; recover the fallen; restore the penitent; remove all hindrances to the advancement of Thy truth; bring all to be of one heart and of one mind within the fold of Thy holy Church; to the honour and glory of Thy Name; through Jesus Christ our Lord. AMEN.

(Adapted from *Prayers, New and Old*)

For the Church

O GOD, Fountain of Light and Truth, give to Thy Church a new vision and a new charity, new wisdom and understanding, that the eternal message of Thy Son, not confused by the traditions of men, may be hailed as the good news of the new age; through Him Who maketh all things new, Jesus Christ our Lord. AMEN.

(*Source unverified*)

Hymn for the Church Militant

LORD, when we cry Thee far and near
And thunder through all lands unknown
The gospel into every ear,
Lord, let us not forget our own.

Cleanse us from ire of creed or class,
The anger of the idle kings;
Sow in our souls, like living grass,
The laughter of all lowly things.

GILBERT KEITH CHESTERTON
(1874–1936)

The City

WHERE cross the crowded ways of life,
  Where sound the cries of race and clan
Above the noise of selfish strife,
  We hear Thy voice, O Son of Man.

In haunts of wretchedness and need,
  On shadowed thresholds dark with fears,
From paths where hide the lures of greed,
  We catch the vision of Thy tears.

From tender childhood's helplessness,
  From woman's grief, man's burdened toil,
From famished souls, from sorrow's stress,
  Thy heart has never known recoil.

The cup of water given for Thee
  Still holds the freshness of Thy grace;
Yet long the multitudes to see
  The sweet compassion of Thy face.

O Master, from the mountain side,
  Make haste to heal these hearts of pain;
Among these restless throngs abide,
  O tread the city's streets again;

Till sons of men shall learn Thy love,
  And follow where Thy feet have trod;
Till glorious from Thy heaven above,
  Shall come the City of our God.

FRANK MASON NORTH

F. SEASONAL DAYS

New Year's Eve

O THOU Who art ever the same, grant us so to pass through the coming year with faithful hearts, that we may be able in all things to please Thy loving eyes; through Jesus Christ our Lord. AMEN.

(*Mozarabic Liturgy*, before 700)

The Lenten Collect

ALMIGHTY and everlasting God, who hatest nothing that thou hast made, and dost forgive the sins of all those who are penitent; Create and make in us new and contrite hearts, that we, worthily lamenting our sins and acknowledging our wretchedness, may obtain of thee, the God of all mercy, perfect remission and forgiveness; through Jesus Christ our Lord. AMEN.

(*The Book of Common Prayer*)

Good Friday

WE implore Thee, by the memory of Thy Cross's hallowed and most bitter anguish, make us fear Thee, make us love Thee, O Christ. AMEN.

ST. BRIDGET (*ca.* 453–523)

St. Bridget is a patron saint of Ireland. Born a slave, she was given her freedom at the request of the King of Leinster, who had been impressed by her piety. She founded a convent on the site of the present town of Kildare.

Good Friday

THEN cometh Jesus with them unto a place called Gethsemane, and saith unto the disciples, Sit ye here, while I go and pray yonder.

And he took with him Peter and the two sons of Zebedee, and began to be sorrowful and very heavy.

Then saith he unto them, My soul is exceeding sorrowful, even unto death: tarry ye here, and watch with me.

And he went a little farther, and fell on his face, and prayed, saying, O my Father, if it be possible, let this cup pass from me: nevertheless not as I will, but as thou wilt.

And he cometh unto the disciples, and findeth them asleep, and saith unto Peter, What, could ye not watch with me one hour?

Watch and pray, that ye enter not into temptation: the spirit indeed is willing, but the flesh is weak.

He went away again the second time, and prayed, saying, O my Father, if this cup may not pass away from me, except I drink it, thy will be done.

And he came and found them asleep again: for their eyes were heavy.

And he left them, and went away again, and prayed the third time, saying the same words.

Then cometh he to his disciples, and saith unto them, Sleep on now, and take your rest: behold, the hour is at hand, and the Son of man is betrayed into the hands of sinners.

Rise, let us be going: behold, he is at hand that doth betray me.

(*Matthew* 26:36–46)

Good Friday

LORD, have mercy upon us.
Christ, have mercy upon us.
Lord, have mercy upon us.

A Litany

Jesus, born in poverty,
born to bring peace among men,
workman at Nazareth,
Have mercy upon us.

Jesus, in whom the proud were scattered and the mighty put down,
giving good things to the hungry,
exalting them of low degree,
Have mercy upon us.

Jesus, in whom all nations of the earth are one,
in whom is neither bond nor free,
brother of all,
Have mercy upon us.

Jesus, preaching good tidings to the poor,
proclaiming release to the captives,
setting at liberty them that are bound,
Have mercy upon us.

Jesus, friend of the poor,
feeder of the hungry,
healer of the sick,
Have mercy upon us.

Jesus, denouncing the oppressor,
instructing the simple,
going about to do good,
Have mercy upon us.

Jesus, teacher of patience,
pattern of gentleness,
prophet of the Kingdom of heaven,
Have mercy upon us.

Jesus, forgiving them that love much,
drawing all men unto thee,
calling them that labor and are heavy laden,
Have mercy upon us.

Jesus, who camest not to be ministered unto, but to minister,
who hadst not where to lay thy head,
loved by the common people,
Have mercy upon us.

Jesus, betrayed for the sake of money,
taken by the chief priests,
condemned by the rulers,
Have mercy upon us.

Jesus, crucified for us,
courageous in suffering,
merciful to thy condemners,
Have mercy upon us.

"A Litany of Labour," in *A Book of Prayers for Students*

Christ's Nativity

I WOULD I were some bird, or star,
Fluttering in woods, or lifted far
  Above this inn,
  And road of sin!
Then either star or bird should be
Shining or singing still to thee.

I would I had in my best part
Fit rooms for thee! or that my heart
  Were so clean as
  Thy manger was!
But I am all filth, and obscene;
Yet, if thou wilt, thou canst make clean.

Sweet Jesu! will then. Let no more
This leper haunt and soil thy door!
  Cure him, ease him,
  O release him!
And let once more, by mystic birth,
The Lord of life be born in earth.

HENRY VAUGHAN

For Christmas

O BLESSED Lord Jesus, give us thankful hearts today for Thee, our choicest gift, our dearest guest.

Let not our souls be busy inns that have no room for Thee and Thine, but quiet homes of prayer and praise where Thou mayest find fit company, where the needful cares of life are wisely ordered and put away, and wide sweet spaces kept for Thee, where holy thoughts pass up and down, and fervent longings watch and wait Thy coming.

So when Thou comest again, O blessed One, mayst Thou find all things ready, and Thy servants waiting for no new master, but one long loved and known.

Even so come, Lord Jesus. AMEN.

(*Source unverified*)

"A MERRY Christmas to us all, my dears. God bless us all!"

Which all the family re-echoed.

"God bless us every one!" said Tiny Tim, the last of all.

CHARLES DICKENS (1812–1870). From "The Christmas Goose at the Cratchits'" (THE CHRISTMAS CAROL)

From "O Little Town of Bethlehem"

O HOLY Child of Bethlehem!
  Descend to us, we pray;
Cast out our sin, and enter in,
  Be born in us to-day.
We hear the Christmas angels
  The great glad tidings tell;
Oh, come to us, abide with us,
  Our Lord Emmanuel!

PHILLIPS BROOKS (1835–1893)

The Fallen

THOSE we have loved the dearest,
  The bravest and the best,
Are summoned from the battle
  To their eternal rest;

There they endure the silence,
  Here we endure the pain—
He that bestows the Valor
  Valor resumes again.

O, Master of all Being,
  Donor of Day and Night,
Of Passion and of Beauty,
  Of Sorrow and Delight,

Thou gav'st them the full treasure
  Of that heroic blend—
The Pride, the Faith, the Courage,
  That holdeth to the end.

Thou gavest us the Knowledge
  Wherein their memories stir—
Master of Life, we thank Thee
  That they were what they were.

DUNCAN CAMPBELL SCOTT

Clean Hands

MAKE this thing plain to us, O Lord!
That not the triumph of the sword—
  Not that alone—can end the strife,
  But reformation of the life—
But full submission to Thy Word!
Not all the stream of blood outpoured
Can Peace—the Long-Desired—afford;
  Not tears of Mother, Maid, or Wife . . .
  Make this thing plain!

We must root out our sins ignored,
By whatsoever name adored;
  Our secret sins, that, ever rife,
  Shrink from the operating knife;
Then shall we rise, renewed, restored . . .
  Make this thing plain!

AUSTIN DOBSON (1840–1921)

XI. "THE LORD BLESS US AND KEEP US"

Benedictions

XI. "THE LORD BLESS US AND KEEP US"

PRAYER is the peace of our spirit, the stillness of our thoughts, the evenness of recollection, the seat of meditation, the rest of our cares, and the calm of our tempest; prayer is the issue of a quiet mind, of untroubled thoughts, it is the daughter of charity and the sister of meekness.

JEREMY TAYLOR (1613–1667)

THE peace of God which passeth all understanding, keep our hearts and minds in the knowledge and love of God, and of His Son Jesus Christ our Lord, and the blessing of God Almighty, the Father, the Son, and the Holy Ghost, be amongst you and remain with you always. AMEN.

(*The Book of Common Prayer*)

The Aaronic Blessing, 1400 B. C.

UNTO God's gracious mercy and protection we commit ourselves. The Lord bless us and keep us. The Lord make His face to shine upon us and be gracious unto us. The Lord lift up the light of His countenance upon us, and give us peace, both now and evermore. AMEN.

(*Numbers* 6:24–26)

GOD bless your coming and going
Through every day!
May grief be behind the hedges
And joy lie along your way.

CATHAL O'BYRNE

Prayer

WHEN the last sea is sailed, when the last shallow's charted,
When the last field is reaped and the last harvest stored,
When the last fire is out and the last guest departed,
Grant the last prayer that I shall pray, Be good to me, O Lord!

And let me pass in a night at sea, a night of storm and thunder,
In the loud crying of the wind through sail and rope and spar;
Send me a ninth great peaceful wave to drown and roll me under
To the cold tunny-fishes' home where the drowned galleons are.

In the dim green quiet place far out of sight and hearing,
Grant I may hear at whiles the wash and thresh of the sea foam
About the fine keen bows of the stately clippers steering
Towards the lone northern star and the fair ports of home.

JOHN MASEFIELD

The Last Invocation

AT the last, tenderly,
From the walls of the powerful, fortressed house,

From the clasp of the knitted locks, from the keep of the well-
closed doors,
Let me be wafted.

Let me glide noiselessly forth;
With the key of softness unlock the locks—with a whisper
Set ope the doors, O soul!

Tenderly—be not impatient!
(Strong is your hold, O mortal flesh!
Strong is your hold, O love!)

WALT WHITMAN

For Blessing

BLESS all who worship Thee, from the rising of the sun unto the going down of the same. Of Thy goodness, give us; with Thy love, inspire us; by Thy spirit, guide us; by Thy power, protect us; in Thy mercy receive us now and always. AMEN.

(*An Ancient Collect,* 440)

St. Paul's Blessing

NOW the God of hope fill you with all joy and peace in believing that ye may abound in hope, through the power of the Holy Ghost.

(*Romans* 15:13)

Benediction

AND now may the blessings of the Lord rest upon all His people in every land, of every tongue. The Lord meet in mercy all that seek Him. The Lord comfort all that suffer and mourn. The Lord hasten His coming, and give us and all His people peace both now and forever more. AMEN.

(*War-Time Prayers*)

O GOD, bless our home, our family, friends, and neighbors, and give us thankful hearts for all thy mercies. AMEN.

(*Prayers, New and Old*)

GOD be gracious unto you, and give you all an heart to serve him, and to do his will, with a good courage and a willing mind; and open your hearts in his law and commandments, and send you peace, and hear your prayers, and be at one with you, and never forsake you in time of trouble. Through Jesus Christ our Lord. AMEN.

(Adapted from *I Maccabees* 1:2–5)

SAVE us, O Lord, while waking and guard us while sleeping; that awake we may watch with Christ, and in peace we may take our rest. AMEN.

(*Anglo-Catholic Prayer Book*)

Benediction

THE Lord Almighty grant us a quiet night and a perfect end; and the blessing of God Almighty, the Father, the Son, and the Holy Ghost, be with us this night and evermore. AMEN.

(*A Chain of Prayers across the Ages*)

NOW unto him that is able to keep you from falling, and to present you faultless before the presence of his glory with exceeding joy,

To the only wise God our Saviour, be glory and majesty, dominion and power, both now and ever. AMEN.

(*Jude* 24–25)

MAY the souls of the faithful, through the mercy of God, rest in peace, and may light perpetual shine upon them; and may the grace of our Lord Jesus Christ, and the love of God, and the fellowship of the Holy Ghost, be with us all evermore. AMEN.

(*Source unverified*)

THE Lord watch between me and thee, when we are absent one from another.

(*Genesis* 31:49)

NOW the God of peace, that brought again from the dead our Lord Jesus, that great Shepherd of the sheep, through the blood of the everlasting covenant,

Make you perfect in every good work to do his will, working in you that which is wellpleasing in his sight, through Jesus Christ; to whom be glory for ever and ever. AMEN.

(*Hebrews* 13:20)

PEACE I leave with you; my peace I give unto you. Not as the world giveth, give I unto you. Let not your heart be troubled, neither let it be afraid.

(*John* 14:27)

APPENDIX

LITURGIES

THE Christian Church from the days of the Apostles has had a fairly definite form of worship commemorating the Last Supper, and at least approximating its institution by our Lord. The first known reference to a written liturgy of the Mass, however, is that of Proclus (d. 446), who tells us that St. Basil, Bishop of Cæsarea in Cappadocia from 370 until his death in 379, *shortened* the liturgy to make it more practicable for the people. From this it would seem that by the middle of the fourth century, if not before, there were written liturgies, and therefore liturgical books of some kind.

As the Church grew, spreading far afield among people of different characteristics and tongues, the Mass came to be celebrated in many variant forms, and almost every diocese developed its own liturgy. Fundamentally these liturgies were the same, differing only in the order of prayers; in the use of vestments, candles, and incense; in length; or in expression. The most interesting and important of them are the following, from many of which prayers used in this book have been taken.

Liturgy of St. James (Greek)—the original, or parent, liturgy of Antioch, believed to have been composed by St. James the Less, Bishop of the Church of Jerusalem, who probably was the "James the Son of Alpheus, Apostle" of the New Testament.

Liturgy of St. Basil (Greek)—still used by the Greek Orthodox Church in Lent.

Liturgy of the Greek Church—correctly, the parent rites of Alexandria and Antioch, and the Byzantine Rite used at Athens and Constantinople, whose original forms in Greek still are extant; reference to the Greek Rite, however commonly means the Byzantine, which next to the Roman is the most widespread of all the liturgies.

Liturgy of St. Mark (Greek)—claimed by the Church of Egypt to be the parent liturgy from which have sprung all others used by Melchites and Copts. According to tradition it is the work of St. Mark, the Evangelist, first Bishop of Alexandria.

Coptic Liturgy of St. Cyril—very much like the Greek Liturgy of St. Mark, with but a few prayers added and all the familiar formulas and greetings left in the original Greek. St. Cyril was the nephew of Theophilus, Patriarch of Alexandria, whom he accompanied to Constantinople in 403 to depose St. John Chrysostom, Patriarch of Constantinople.

Leonine Sacramentary—the oldest extant Sacramentary of the Roman Rite. Only one manuscript of it is known, written in the seventh century and attributed, rather questionably, to St. Leo I (440–461).

Gelasian Sacramentary—exists in several manuscripts, the oldest of them a book used at the Abbey of St. Denis in Paris in the seventh or early eighth century. A ninth-century tradition claims that it is the work of Pope Gelasius I (492–496), but it is more generally believed to have been written in the sixth, or possibly even the seventh, century.

Gallican Sacramentary—the name Gallican is given to the rite in use in Gaul from about the fifth century to the end of the eighth. It may have been of Oriental origin, brought to Milan by the Cappadocian Auxentius, who was Bishop there from 355 to 374, and spreading from Milan into Gaul, Spain, and Britain. More likely it originated in Rome. There are no manuscripts extant earlier than the end of the seventh century.

Gregorian Sacramentary—between 781 and 791 the Emperor Charlemagne, wishing to introduce the Roman Rite into his kingdom, wrote to Pope Adrian I asking for a service book of that Rite.

In sending it, Adrian wrote that the book had been composed "by our holy predecessor, the divinely speaking Pope Gregory" (590–604). It was not the actual liturgy of St. Gregory, however, that Adrian sent, but the current use of Rome. This book, supplemented from the Gelasian Sacramentary and from Gallican sources, became the Gregorian Sacramentary.

Roman Breviary—between the ninth and eleventh centuries the Gregorian Sacramentary, with its Gelasian and Gallican additions, found its way back to Rome, supplanted the original Roman Rite, and became the foundation of the present Roman Missal. Distinct from the Missal is the Roman Breviary, which, divided into four sections according to the seasons of the year, contains the canonical or day hours and certain special Offices.

Sarum Use—one of the earliest well-known uses in Britain was the "Sarum Use" compiled by St. Osmund, a Norman nobleman who had come to England with William the Conqueror and had been made Bishop of Sarum (Salisbury) by him in 1078. The Sarum Use spread rapidly through England and was followed even in the Archdiocese of Canterbury. From it was taken much of the present service of the Church of England.

Mozarabic Rite—used generally in Spain and Portugal until the latter half of the eleventh century, and still used in certain churches in Toledo at regular intervals.

Jacobite Liturgy—the rite used by the Jacobite sect in Syria. It is simply the Antiochene liturgy translated from the Greek into the Syriac language.

Russian Liturgy—the Liturgy of St. Basil translated into Old Slavonic.

These notes are based largely on articles in THE CATHOLIC ENCYCLOPEDIA *and the* ENCYCLOPEDIA BRITANNICA.

IF WE traverse the world, it is possible to find cities without walls, without letters, without kings, without wealth, without coin, without schools and theaters; but a city without a temple, or that practiseth not worship, prayers, and the like, no one ever saw.

PLUTARCH (50–120 A.D.)

INDEX OF FIRST LINES

A

B

C

D

E

F

G

J

K

L

M

P

Q

S

T

U

W

Y

Z

GENERAL INDEX

A

B

C

D

E

F

G

H

I

J

M

N

O

P

Q

R

S

T

U

V

W

Y

Z